Moral Relativism

New Dialogues in Philosophy

A series in dialogue form, explicating foundational problems in the philosophy of existence, knowledge, and value

SERIES EDITOR

Professor Dale Jacquette, Senior Professorial Chair in Theoretical Philosophy, University of Bern, Switzerland

In the tradition of Plato, Berkeley, Hume, and other great philosophical dramatists, Rowman & Littlefield presents an exciting new series of philosophical dialogues. This innovative series has been conceived to encourage a deeper understanding of philosophy through the literary device of lively argument in scripted dialogues, a pedagogic method that is proven effective in helping students to understand challenging concepts while demonstrating the merits and shortcomings of philosophical positions displaying a wide variety of structure and content. Each volume is compact and affordable, written by a respected scholar whose expertise informs each dialogue, and presents a range of positions through its characters' voices that will resonate with students' interests while encouraging them to engage in philosophical dialogue themselves.

TITLES

J. Kellenberger, *Moral Relativism: A Dialogue* (2008)
Michael Ruse, *Evolution and Religion: A Dialogue* (2008)
Charles Taliaferro, *Dialogues About God* (2008)

FORTHCOMING TITLES

Bradley Dowden, *The Metaphysics of Time: A Dialogue*
Dale Jacquette, *Dialogues on the Ethics of Capital Punishment* (2009)
Michael Krausz, *Relativism: A Dialogue*
Dan Lloyd, *Ghosts in the Machine: A Dialogue*
Brian Orend, *On War: A Dialogue* (2009)

Moral Relativism

A Dialogue

J. Kellenberger

ROWMAN & LITTLEFIELD PUBLISHERS, INC.
Lanham • Boulder • New York • Toronto • Plymouth, UK

ROWMAN & LITTLEFIELD PUBLISHERS, INC.

Published in the United States of America
by Rowman & Littlefield Publishers, Inc.
A wholly owned subsidary of The Rowman & Littlefield Publishing Group, Inc.
4501 Forbes Boulevard, Suite 200, Lanham, Maryland 20706
www.rowmanlittlefield.com

Estover Road
Plymouth PL6 7PY
United Kingdom

British Library Cataloguing in Publication Information Available

Library of Congress Cataloging-in-Publication Data

The hardback edition of this book was previously cataloged by the Library of
Congress as follows:

Kellenberger, J.
    Moral relativism : a dialogue / J. Kellenberger.
        p. cm. — (New dialogues in philosophy)
    Includes bibliographical references and index.
    1. Ethical relativism. I. Title.
BJ37.K45 2008
171'.7—dc22   2007050754

    ISBN-13: 978-0-7425-4773-5 (cloth : alk. paper)
    ISBN-10: 0-7425-4773-6 (cloth : alk. paper)
    ISBN-13: 978-0-7425-4774-2 (pbk. : alk. paper)
    ISBN-10: 0-7425-4774-4 (pbk. : alk. paper)
    eISBN-13: 978-0-7425-6463-3
    eISBN-10: 0-7425-6463-0

Printed in the United States of America

♾™ The paper used in this publication meets the minimum requirements of
American National Standard for Information Sciences—Permanence of Paper
for Printed Library Materials, ANSI/NISO Z39.48-1992.

To Anne

Contents

Contents

Preface

Relativism, it seems, is in the air. It is in the intellectual air we breath. Although relativism may take many forms, relating itself to concepts, religion, and even truth, moral relativism has an immediacy for all of us who are moral beings. This is to say that it has an immediacy for all of us human beings, for like it or not we all operate in the moral sphere, making decisions about what we ought to do and what we ought not to do. Moral relativism has implications for each moral breath we take.

Many today are aware of the pervasive presence of the idea of moral relativism, and it is not uncommon to encounter expressions of concern about moral relativism, just as it is not uncommon to find affirmations and condemnations of moral relativism in one quarter or another. This, however, does not mean that there is complete agreement about what moral relativism says. In fact there is not.

In this dialogue the participants will discuss and test several definitions of moral relativism. Some of the participants will favor one or another form of moral relativism, and others will raise objections and argue against moral relativism. In the course of their discussion the participants will confront several questions. They include: If morality is relative, what is it relative *to*? Is morality objective? And what does *objective* mean? Are there moral universals? If there are, what does that mean for moral relativism? What is the significance of cultural differences for moral relativism? How does moral relativism relate to religion?

The eight participants carry on their dialogue over the course of several weeks, meeting six times. Each meeting corresponds to one of the six chapters, and each meeting finds them facing new dimensions of the issue of moral relativism.

Several people have helped in the shaping and publication of this volume. In particular I wish to think Ross Miller, Senior Editor at Rowman & Littlefield, Dale Jacquette, the Series Editor of New Dialogues in Philosophy, who read an earlier draft of the dialogue and offered many valuable suggestions, and Elaine McGarraugh, Production Editor at Rowman & Littlefield.

1

⌀

Subjectivism, Some Cultural Differences, and Cultural Moral Relativism

SETTING: Sam's apartment. Sam, Sarah, Andrew, Zainab, Yusuf, and Maria are in the living room. Sam answers a knock at the door.

Sam: Well, hello, Jerry. Please come in.

Jerry: Hello, Sam. Hello everyone. Let me introduce Mr. Vishnu McGregor. He and his wife live across the street from me. Mr. McGregor, meet Sam and Sarah, and Maria and Andrew. Sam and Sarah and I went to the same college.

Vishnu: I am pleased to meet all of you. As far as I am concerned first names are fine. Please call me "Vishnu."

Sam: Glad to meet you, Vishnu.

Zainab: Hello, Jerry. It is good to see you again and to meet Vishnu. Let me introduce my cousin Yusuf, who is visiting from Pakistan.

Sam: We were discussing a very interesting film that we all have just seen, *The Decision.*

Jerry: I saw it the other night. Well done for the most part, I thought.

Vishnu: I am afraid that I haven't seen it. What is it about?

1

Sarah: It's set in France in the 1940s during World War II, when Paris was occupied by the Nazis. The main character is a Parisian, a young man named Jean-Louis, who has to make a hard decision. Paris is under the thumb of the Nazis, and some of the French are keeping a low profile and making the best of it for themselves, but others are leaving France by a kind of underground railway and joining the French resistance army in England.

Sam: So one thing that Jean-Louis can do is go to England and join the French army; and he wants to do it. But there is a problem. He lives with his mother, and his mother depends on him a lot, both materially and emotionally. If he leaves her, he is afraid that she will come to grief. It doesn't help matters that she hates the Germans and has a tendency to be outspoken.

Jerry: So Jean-Louis has a dilemma. He can come to the aid of his country and possibly put his mother at risk. Or he can provide a son's support to his mother, and not answer the call to defend his country. I liked the way the film made each alternative strong in its appeal. Good acting, and the directing was really effective. I was a little disappointed with the ending, though.

Andrew: You mean how Jean-Louis at the end is standing on the street late at night under a street light all alone and undecided?

Sam: The camera zooms out, and we don't know what he decided.

Vishnu: I have not seen the film, but your description reminds me very much of Jean-Paul Sartre's essay *Existentialism is a Humanism*, which he wrote in 1946. In that essay Sartre gives us the case of a hard moral decision that one of his students had to make, and it was just like the decision in the film. As in the film, it was the time of World War II back in the 1940s, and Sartre and his student were in Nazi-occupied France. Sartre's student also had to decide between staying in France and taking care of his mother, and going to England and joining the Free French Forces to fight the occupiers.

Sarah: Well, that's right. I remember that Sam and I had a class in which we read Sartre's essay. I wonder why Sartre wasn't mentioned in the credits.

Jerry: I think I had the same class. As I recall, Sartre does not tell us what his student should do or even what he decided.

Zainab: I too have read Sartre's essay, and you are right, Jerry. All Sartre says is that his student is the one who is faced with the choice and he must choose.

Sam: I want to say the same thing about Sartre's student as I would about Jean-Louis. It seems to me that Sartre's student could have done either and done what is right provided he made a sincere choice. And if there were two young men faced with his decision, one could have stayed with his mother and the other could have joined the Free French Forces. Both would have done what was right if each had made a sincere choice. It seems to me that morality is relative in this way.

Vishnu: People unavoidably have to make their own moral decisions and moral choices, just as they have to make their own moral judgments about what they are morally required to do or what is morally permissible or wrong. Even if they ask another person *they* have to choose to accept that other person's moral advice or judgment. Are you saying more than that individuals have to make their own moral choices?

Sam: Yes, I am saying that if an individual makes a sincere choice, one that reflects his or her moral feelings or beliefs, then he or she will be doing what is morally right.

Maria: That sounds like a dangerous thought to me. Pope Benedict said relativism is "letting oneself be swept along by every wind of teaching" and he said that today "we are moving toward a dictatorship of relativism, which does not recognize any thing as for certain and which has as its highest goal one's own ego and one's own desire."

Sarah: I think that Rabbi Meyer at our temple might well agree with Pope Benedict's warning about relativism.

Sam: Pope Benedict's concern does not seem to apply to the student's moral decision; it may not be his desire to stay with his mother, yet he may do this because he feels it is right.

Jerry: I recognize that people have moral feelings and that Sartre's student *could* feel that he should stay with his mother in France, just as he *could* feel that he should join the Free French Forces. But it is not just his moral feeling that determines what is morally right for him to do. There are objective moral reasons that relate to his decision. I believe that morality is not relative; it's objective.

Vishnu: Jerry, what do you mean by "objective"?

Jerry: When something is true objectively it does not depend on what people feel or believe or choose; it is true irrespective of whether you or I believe it or like it. For instance, it is an objective fact that there are coffee cups before us on this table.

Sam: What I mean when I say that morality is relative is not that everything is relative; if morality is relative, still many facts about the world will be objective in your sense. It remains objectively true that bricks or books dropped from a third story window will fall to earth, that fire burns, and that dogs are mammals—and that there are coffee cups on this table. People believing that the world was flat did not make it flat. In fact if it's true that morality is relativistic, that will be an objective truth. It's just that it's not objectively true that something I do is right or wrong, because the rightness or wrongness of what I do does depend on what "people" feel or believe. It depends on what I feel or believe.

Jerry: Sartre also says that when we choose something as a value for ourselves, we choose it as a value for everyone. When I choose an "image" of myself, a certain way of life, then I am choosing that way of life as a value for everyone.

Vishnu: Yes, I remember that part of Sartre's essay. It would be understandable if Sartre were saying simply that when I choose a way of life I am recommending *its consideration* to others. Sartre, however, seems to be making a much stronger claim. He says that in creating the man we want to be we are creating an image of man as "he ought to be." He is thinking this, it seems, because, as he sees it, every time we choose to be this or that we affirm the value of what we choose. This means, for Sartre, that, "we always choose the better," as he says, and he adds "nothing can be better for us unless it is better for all." So he ends up with the idea that each of our way-of-life choices makes it a value for all other "men," and presumably he means all other persons. It has always seemed to me that this is a curious thing for him to hold. His example, or one of them, involves marriage. Sartre is fairly clear that if I choose getting married and having a family as a value for myself, then I am choosing it as a value for everyone. But that does not seem right. I may appreciate that it is better for some people to remain single. And consider the other side of the coin. Take the example of a man who chooses to become a Catholic priest. He may value that way of life for himself. However, is he thereby recommending it for every other man? Of course not!

Jerry: And I don't suppose Sartre could say that the man who chooses to become a Catholic priest is choosing that as a value for *everyone*. It could hardly be a value for women. Not as things are now in the Catholic Church.

Vishnu: There is another problem for Sartre. Say that one person chooses to marry and have a family and another chooses to become a priest, or a nun, taking a vow of celibacy. Does that mean that each becomes a way of life for all of us that we all ought to follow? Of course it would be impossible to follow both since they conflict and are incompatible.

Sam: I was thinking that if I sincerely choose to do something, or believe or feel it is right, then it is right *for me*. I wasn't thinking that my choice or feeling would make it right for everyone. Others may have very different feelings.

Vishnu: Good for you, Sam! Your emendation takes care of the internal problem with Sartre's subjectivism. In fact, with your emendation, we get a standard subjectivism, which makes morality relative to each individual. Its basic claims are that, first, what the individual feels or believes, or chooses, makes what she or he does right, and, second, the individual's feelings or beliefs or choices make it right for her or him, but not for the next person. So, going back to the example of Sartre's student, if he feels that, say, joining the Free French Forces is right, then it is right for him, and of course if he feels it is wrong, then it is wrong for him. But it is the feelings of the next person, or his beliefs or choices, that will make joining the Free French Forces right or wrong for him.

Sam: So the understanding of morality that seems right to me is what Vishnu just called "standard subjectivism." And I am happy in saying that it is "objectively true." If it is, then I think that we can answer the concerns expressed by Pope Benedict. As Sarah expressed them, he was concerned that those following relativism would not accept anything as certain and would end up doing just as they desire. But, going back to what I said before, a person who does what she or he feels or believes is right may not be doing what she or he desires to do. Putting myself in the place of Sartre's student, I may *want* to stay at home supporting my mother, where it is safe and sound, and yet feel that the right thing to do is to join the Free French Forces. To put it another way, subjectivists can be tempted to do what they want to do when they know it is wrong because it is not what they feel is right. In the same way Pope Benedict's other concern can be answered. If I can know my own feelings or beliefs about what is right or wrong, then I can be certain about what is right or wrong—right or wrong for me, of course. But, if subjectivism is correct, then rightness and wrongness for the individual are what moral rightness and wrongness really are.

Maria: I don't think that that can be right. If I feel that it is morally all right to drive over the speed limit, then is it going to be morally all right for me to do it? It can't be. It's illegal.

Jerry: Maria, I think there are problems with Sam's view that he has yet to face, but there is a reply to your objection that Sam as a subjectivist can make. Subjectivism is a view about the nature of morality—what makes our actions right or wrong—not a view on the law and what makes our actions legal or illegal. I believe that there is such a distinction, and it is important. So it is a plus for Sam's subjectivism that it can recognize it.

Sarah: And what if I feel it is all right to steal from my neighbors, won't that affect them?

Jerry: Sure it will. But the effects of our actions are not relevant to the morality of our actions, a careful and consistent subjectivist has to say. If they were relevant we would have an objective criterion for morality. The most a subjectivist can say is that when *he* or *she* sees that his or her action would hurt someone, then he or she begins to feel it is wrong and that feeling makes it wrong for him or her to do it. Of course the subjectivist also has to say that if someone else has a perverse and sadistic streak and feels that it is right to inflict pain on others, then it is just as right for this other person to do so as it is wrong for him or her to do such a thing.

Sam: I see what you are saying, Jerry. Let me think about it.

Vishnu: There is something else to think about here. Sam, you say that moral rightness and wrongness depend on what people feel or believe, and what is right for you depends on what you feel or believe. Let's say that morality is relative because it depends on what people feel or believe. If we accept this much, there is a question that presents itself. That question is: To what person or persons is morality relative? Is it relative to the individual or is it relative to a culture or society?

Andrew: Well, it seems quite clear that what people like and what people value can vary from one culture to another. I am from Nigeria, and there are things that people like in Nigeria that people here in America, with few exceptions, would not like at all.

Yusuf: And sometimes what people in one culture like or value is found to be repulsive in another society.

Andrew: I would guess that each of us could name at least one thing that was valued somewhere in some culture that he or she found odd, upsetting, or even deeply repulsive.

Sarah: One thing I find really strange is eating insects, not that I have actually seen it. Eating insects is not allowed by Jewish dietary laws, and so it would be wrong for me to eat any insect. But, moreover, I find it strange and revolting; so even if the dietary laws allowed it, I would never be tempted to eat an insect. Yet I understand that in Japan you can order different insects fried or boiled from restaurant menus.

Andrew: In parts of Nigeria termites and grasshoppers are cooked and eaten. I very much like roasted grasshoppers.

Maria: In Mexico, too, insects are eaten, and they are sold in the markets. In southern Mexico, people eat green caterpillars—*cuchamas*—when they are in season. This is a centuries-old practice. And I have heard that fried caterpillars are served in expensive restaurants. I have never tried them.

Zainab: Islam also has dietary laws. Often they are close to the Jewish laws, but while most insects are forbidden, the dietary laws of Islam allow grasshoppers to be eaten. It is allowable for me to eat grasshoppers, but I have never been tempted to and have never been offered such a morsel. Like Sarah, and unlike Andrew, I find the idea of eating any insect quite distasteful.

Vishnu: *"Chacun à son goût,"* as the French say. "Each to his or her own taste." Here it seems to apply.

Sam: My example would have to be infanticide. Infanticide, female infanticide in particular, was widely practiced in China, and is still practiced there. Also, if I remember correctly, infanticide was practiced in Eskimo—or, as we say now, Inuit—societies. I find this practice shocking and cruel beyond measure. These are my moral feelings about the practice. And, yes, I see that as a subjectivist I have to say that if any parent feels killing his or her baby is right, then it is right for him or her to do so. I concede that I have some thinking to do about this.

Maria: My example is something I find strange in a sense. Not because I am unfamiliar with it. And not because I cannot understand it. I find not eating pork and not eating beef to be something very strange. Here is why I do. At my house on Saturdays we have a special breakfast of Mexican pork sausage with potatoes and eggs, *chorizo con papas y huevos*. The family comes together for that breakfast. It creates a special time of intimacy; and sometimes at night we will have *tamales* that my grandmother has made. Each time that good food seems to open the way to family communication and intimacy. If we did not eat pork and beef we could not have *chorizo* or *tamales*; and that would mean our family life would be different—not impoverished, but lacking a significant occasion for coming together. I appreciate that in other cultures, and within our broader American culture, there are traditional Jews and Muslims who do not eat pork and traditional Hindus who do not eat beef; and of course there is family intimacy in these communities, but it is hard for me to imagine. Maybe if I knew their traditional dishes, it would be easier for me.

Sarah: My family keeps kosher, so we of course do not eat pork or even have it in the house. However our Shabbat dinners on Friday nights are a time for religious observance and also for a kind of boisterous family intimacy. We have plenty of food—fish and chicken—and sometimes my mother will make ratzelech, a wonderful potato pancake that defies description it's so good. It is just like what Maria was saying, only the food is different.

Vishnu: My turn? Here is my example: using a skull cup, a cup made from a human cranium, as a ritualistic drinking cup. Skull cups are used in certain Buddhist rituals in Tibet, something I discovered when I was working on an engineering project in Tibet several years ago. In India the Hindu goddess Kali is represented with a necklace of human skulls, and I have seen a European religious painting showing St. Francis kneeling in prayer with a skull used as *memento mori*, a reminder of death. But I was unprepared for the ritualistic use of a human cranium that I found in Tibet.

Andrew: One might compare this to Christian scripture and liturgy. I can imagine some Buddhists being taken aback to find that in the New Testament Jesus Christ says he is the bread of life and those who eat his flesh and drink his blood will have eternal life. I am Anglican, and these very words are taken from the New Testament and used in the liturgy for Holy Communion, in which a wafer—representing Christ's body—and wine—representing Christ's blood—are consumed by the congregation.

Sarah: I don't know about the reaction of those who are Buddhists, but those of us in the Jewish tradition would have a strong aversion to such a thing, even understood symbolically. The consumption of blood—any blood—is absolutely forbidden by the dietary laws.

Zainab: Islamic dietary laws also forbid the consumption of blood. So for Muslims too the Christian ritual would seem strange and upsetting. However, the example I would present is the example of what is sometimes called female circumcision or female genital mutilation. This is the practice of cutting or cutting away the clitoris and much of the external female genitalia from young women and girls. This practice is found in several cultures, and it is more than strange or odd to me. I find it horrifically morally wrong.

Jerry: I want to give two examples, both of which I have come across in my reading over the past couple of weeks. They both are strikingly different from what occurs in my culture, the mainstream American culture. And they are very different from each other. My first example is standing very close to someone in conversation or in an elevator, as I understand is done in Italy, for instance. If someone I was talking to got very close to me—his face in my face—I would feel uncomfortable. If I lived in Italy I suppose I'd get used to it. My second example is different and different in kind. In some parts of the world, in the Arab world and the Gulf region, there occur what are called "honor killings." A daughter who becomes pregnant before marriage or refuses to enter an arranged marriage, or a wife who seeks a divorce, or a female member of a family who is the victim of a sexual assault, may be killed by the male members of the family for the sake of the family's "honor." This practice is often against the law in the countries where it occurs, but if there is any punishment at all it is lenient. Culturally these murders are approved of. It is this approval that I find worse than strange. To use Zainab's expression, I find it horrifically morally wrong.

Zainab: The practice of "honor killing" is found in some Muslim cultures, and sometimes it is said to be sanctioned by Islam by those who confuse their cultural heritage with Islam. Islamic scholars condemn the practice. It clearly goes against the teachings of Islam.

Andrew: My example is something that I found strange in this culture, the American mainstream culture. Here if people need to go two blocks to the store to get a loaf of bread they get in their cars and drive there. To me this is extraordinary. In Nigeria we would walk.

Yusuf: I have an example similar to Andrew's. I would give the following example of something that strikes me as strange and upsetting. It is the way young women dress in America. So much is exposed. They go in public with bare arms and often with much of their legs uncovered. Sometimes they even have bare midriffs. I had seen American women dressed in this way in Hollywood movies, but still I was unprepared for it on the actual streets and campuses of America. The contrast with how women dress in Pakistan is very great. In Pakistan such dress would be immodest in the extreme. I struggle to understand how such dress can be regarded as modest.

Vishnu: In the light of this array of cultural differences let me repeat the question I asked before. If morality is relative to what persons believe or feel or choose, to what person or persons is morality relative? Is it relative to the individual, as you say, Sam, and as subjectivism says, or is it relative to a culture or society? This is a question for Sam, but also for the rest of us.

Jerry: Well, it isn't a question for me because I don't think that morality is relative to what people believe or feel. I can see, though, that it is a question that can come up inside relativism. For Sartre in *Existentialism is a Humanism*, or at least for "standard subjectivism," morality is relative to the individual, determined by his or her beliefs or feelings or choices—some personal attitude.

But why couldn't some other relativist think that morality is relative to what a society or culture believes or accepts—some cultural attitude?

Vishnu: And in fact there have been those who have said that moral rightness and wrongness are relative to cultures or societies. Some anthropologists have maintained that their anthropological fieldwork has established that morality is relative to cultures. These anthropologists thought that cultures determine very much indeed: how people in a culture dress, how they season their food, how directions from one place to another are given, the musical scale used in the culture, how gender is understood, and so on. But importantly some thought that cultures determine not just these values but their own moralities as well.

Sarah: In my sophomore year, I had Anthro 101. I remember we read about Ruth Benedict, Franz Boas, and other anthropologists; and we discussed cultural relativism.

Vishnu: Both Franz Boas and Ruth Benedict, who was his student, made important and lasting contributions to anthropology. Another student of Franz Boas was Melville Herskovits and he also was an influential twentieth-century anthropologist. I was thinking of him in particular. When I was a young man I once heard him give a lecture at Northwestern University in Illinois. He held that societies or cultures "set up" their own values, and that the values "set up" by a society then provide a guide for that society. Herskovits called this view "cultural relativism." As it applies to morality it is "cultural moral relativism," and it says that, first, societies or cultures "set up" or define their moral values; and, second, a culture's values determine what is right and wrong within that culture, but not outside it.

Yusuf: It seems that cultural moral relativism is parallel to subjectivism.

Vishnu: That's right. For subjectivism, individuals create their own moral values by choices, feelings, or beliefs or by some individual attitude, and an individual's created values determine what is morally right or wrong for that individual; whereas for cultural moral relativism, societies or cultures create their own moral values or codes, and their created values determine what is right or wrong for the members of a particular society.

Sam: So for cultural moral relativism morality is limited to a society.

Vishnu: You might say that, but in a way, for cultural moral relativism, morality is not limited to the society. Yes, for cultural moral relativism, a society's values determine what is right or wrong for only the members of that society, but the actions of those members may affect members of other societies. For instance, in many societies it is a cultural requirement that hospitality be given to guests from other societies. And sometimes the actions expected of a society's members by a society can greatly affect the members of other societies. In the past in headhunting societies, men would raid other tribes, taking the heads of those they killed as trophies or sources of power. Head-hunting was practiced by various social groups in different parts of the world. For instance, it was practiced by the Jivaro in the upper Amazon, and it was a practice in Papua, New Guinea. For cultural moral relativism it would be morally acceptable, even required, for the members of these societies to raid other communities and take the heads of those they killed as prizes or amulets if the practice was approved or demanded by their head-hunting society. The same point, or an analogous point, holds for subjectivism, as Sarah saw. If an individual feels that an action that affects others, like stealing from them, is right, then it is right for that individual, even if others are hurt. If Sartre's student feels it is right to join the Free French Forces, then that will be the right thing for him to do, subjectivism would say, and of course in doing this he will be taking up arms against others.

Sarah: I am glad that I don't live in a head-hunting society. Still, all considered, if I had to choose between subjectivism and cultural moral relativism, the cultural view seems better. If individuals could define morality for themselves, we'd have chaos.

Vishnu: It is interesting that you would say that. Herskovits had a similar concern, and he rejected individual relativism. He thought that following the moral code of one's society was necessary for "regularity in life," as he put it.

Jerry: I think that subjectivism is chaotic in another way too. It is chaotic in that if two subjectivists disagreed on a moral question there would be no way for them to settle their disagreement.

Sam: But isn't that just the way it is when two people disagree about what is the morally right thing to do or the morally right way to proceed?

Jerry: Often, I suppose, moral disagreements do not get settled. This is true especially regarding the big issues, like abortion or the rightness of a war. At the same time, though, people sometimes bring forward relevant points to support their moral claims. The thing about subjectivism is that, if it is correct, there would be no possible way to support one's moral claim or to settle a moral disagreement, not even *in principle*. The chaos I see entailed by subjectivism is the chaos that is the opposite of reasoned human discourse. If subjectivism were correct, there could be shouting or sullen silence, but no reasoned discourse.

Sam: Why do you think that there can be no reasoning between two subjectivists who disagree?

Jerry: Let's imagine two subjectivists who disagree about cheating on their income tax. One says that it is all right, and the other says it is wrong. If subjectivism is correct, it *is* all right for the first subjectivist to cheat on his income tax if he feels it is all right, and, at the same time, it *is* wrong for the second subjectivist to cheat on her income tax if she feels it is wrong. What is there to talk about? Will one say to the other "You do not really feel that way"? "Yes, I do," the other will say, and that is the end of it. It is not relevant to argue that the one's not paying his income tax increases the burden on others, and it is not relevant to argue that the income tax brackets are not fair. Neither fact is the slightest evidence against the claim "This is the way I feel." And for subjectivism it is how you feel that determines what is right or wrong.

Vishnu: It is hard to argue with Jerry's point. Furthermore, it is not necessary for his criticism that it be two subjectivists that disagree. If subjectivism is correct, then everyone's morality is determined by what she or he feels, not just the morality of those who accept subjectivism. As Sam said, if subjectivism is true it is objectively true.

However, there is something the subjectivist could draw to our attention. It is true that, for subjectivism, pointing out that one's not paying the amount of income tax that one owes will increase the burden on others is not relevant to the truth of the moral claim that it is all right to cheat on one's income tax. Still it could be a factor in changing the moral feeling of the person who feels it is all right to cheat on one's income tax. This a subjectivist could consistently hold.

Sam: Very good. Thank you, Vishnu.

Jerry: Yes, I see that. Notice, though, that for subjectivism it doesn't matter *how* one's moral feelings are changed. We could cite facts, or we could use hypnosis. If I understand subjectivism, it doesn't matter.

Sam: I, for one, do not feel it would be right to use hypnosis to change someone's mind, or drugs either.

Jerry: And so it would be wrong for you to use hypnosis or drugs. But for subjectivism itself it does not matter how minds and moral feelings are changed. Now that I think of it, isn't there something funny about two subjectivists, or any two people under the subjectivist scenario, having a moral disagreement in the first place? If all I am saying in saying that doing something is right is that *I* feel it is right, and all you are doing in saying that thing is wrong is saying that *you* feel it is wrong, where is the disagreement?

Andrew: It seems to me that these points, or ones very close to them, apply to cultural moral relativism as well. If subjectivism is chaotic in the sense that it rules out any role for reasoned discourse to address moral disagreements, so is cultural moral relativism. If all that members of Society A are doing in saying that something is right is saying that Society A says it is right or approves of it, and all members of Society B are doing in saying that something is wrong is saying that Society B says it is wrong or disapproves of it, again where is the disagreement? And if we allowed there is a disagreement, given what cultural moral relativism maintains, once it was clear that Society A said something was right and Society B said it was wrong, there would be nothing more to say. Further facts would not be relevant to the issue of rightness or wrongness.

Sarah: So subjectivism is chaotic in Jerry's sense in that it gives no place to reasoned discourse when there is moral disagreement, if it allows for moral disagreement at all; but cultural moral relativism is also chaotic in this sense. However, it remains that subjectivism does not provide guidance and regularity in our lives, while following the moral code of one's society does. It remains that *in this sense*, as Herskovits saw, subjectivism is chaotic and cultural moral relativism is not. So it does seem that cultural moral relativism is preferable. And it is supported by anthropology.

Maria: Does cultural moral relativism have a basis in anthropological fact?

Vishnu: Some have thought so. They have argued that the findings of anthropologists investigating different cultures or societies have established that morality differs from culture to culture and is relative to cultures. They noted that in one culture it was considered morally allowable for a man to have more than one wife, while in others it was not considered morally allowable. In fact Herskovits himself observed that in Dahomey, now Benin, in West Africa, the family unit consisted of one husband and several wives. Many other differences in various societal "moral codes" or moral beliefs have been noted. Headhunting, as I observed, is approved of in some societies, but not in all, of course. An early example is one Herodotus noted more than two thousand years ago. He reported on the different ways the Greeks and the Callatians treat their dead fathers. The Greeks burned the bodies of their fathers and the Callatians, in his account, ate the bodies of their dead fathers. (Parenthetically, Herodotus terms the Callatians "Indians." They are quite unrepresentative Indians. Today in India, and for many centuries, back to the time of Herodotus and before, cremation, the practice Herodotus attributes to the Greeks, is and has been the common Hindu practice.) But back to Herodotus' account. Herodotus reported that the Greeks were appalled by the practice of Callatians, and the Callatians were appalled by the practice of the Greeks. And these examples could be multiplied. Some societies have allowed infanticide, as Sam noted. Others, like the dominant American and European societies, would never allow it.

Yusuf: What do these different moral beliefs in different cultures prove?

Vishnu: As I say, several have thought they prove that cultural moral relativism is true.

Jerry: I don't see that. Granting that all these reports about different moral beliefs in different cultures are correct, what rules out some of these societies or cultures just being wrong or mistaken in their moral beliefs?

Vishnu: That is precisely the flaw in the reasoning that has been identified by some.

Sarah: But who is to say which, if any, society is mistaken in its moral beliefs?

Vishnu: That is an important question. On what basis can we or anyone judge a society's moral belief to be wrong or right? However, the flaw in the reasoning is that it does not *rule out* that societies might be mistaken in their moral beliefs. To see this flaw one need only look at the reasoning and observe that this possibility is not denied by it. One need not provide the basis for judging which cultural moral beliefs are mistaken in order to point out that the reasoning does not rule out the possibility that some cultures or societies hold mistaken moral beliefs. Even a committed cultural moral relativist can observe that there is this hole in the reasoning offered in support of cultural moral relativism.

Sarah: Can't we just add to the reasoning that no culture is mistaken in its moral beliefs?

Jerry: We, or those reasoning this way, could make this addition. But if they did, they would beg the question.

Sarah: What's that? What is "begging the question"?

Jerry: You beg the question when without additional support you simply assume in your reasoning what nobody will accept unless they *already* accept what you are trying to prove. The only people who will accept that no culture or society is ever mistaken in its moral beliefs are cultural moral relativists. A gross example of begging the question is arguing that cultural moral relativism is true *because* morality is relative to cultures. Such reasoning simply assumes going in what is to be proven. In the same way, if less evidently, simply assuming that no culture is mistaken in its moral beliefs begs the question against all those who question cultural moral relativism.

Sam: So it looks as though cultural moral relativism is wrong after all.

Vishnu: We cannot conclude that cultural moral relativism is wrong from the fact—allowing that it is a fact—that this reasoning offered in its support does not prove it is true. It could still be right, or true, even though this reasoning does not show that it is true. The most that we can observe is that *this* reasoning does not establish that it is the right view of morality.

Jerry: I can see that, Vishnu. And of course what you say allows that cultural moral relativism could be wrong, as I confess I think it is. But at the same time I think I see an advantage that cultural moral relativism has over subjectivism. Sam argued that subjectivism could answer Pope Benedict's concerns about relativism because it allows us to be certain about what is right and does not make pursuing our desires right. Pursuing any one of our desires may not be right for subjectivism because there is a difference between desiring something and feeling or believing that it is right. Cultural moral relativism also answers Pope Benedict's concerns because we can often be certain about what our culture's moral attitudes are, and following the moral dictates of our culture is distinguishable from following our own desires. What our culture says is right and our personal desires might often diverge. So here too subjectivism and cultural moral relativism seem to be parallel. But I see a significant difference. For subjectivism, if individuals could somehow change their moral feelings or beliefs, so that they came to feel that what they desired was all right after all, *then*, given what subjectivism says, it would in that instant become right or all right for them. Individuals' changing their minds about how they feel or what they believe is right is a psychological matter. Maybe they could talk themselves into it. To change what is morally right or morally allowable, given what cultural moral relativism says, is a lot harder. One would have to change one's culture's moral attitude, and that is a bigger task than just changing one's mind. So maybe there is something to what Herskovits and Sarah say. There is more moral stability provided by the cultural form of moral relativism than by subjectivism. But I still think both are wrong.

2

⁘

A Remembered Incident, Human Rights as a "Higher Standard," and Arguments against Cultural Moral Relativism

SETTING: Sam's apartment a few days later. The entire group is present. There is a loud knock on the door, and Sam goes to answer it.

Sam: Well, Shawn, how are you, man? Come in.

Shawn: Thanks. Hey, what is this? A party?

Sam: No, not exactly. Want a beer?

Shawn: Yeah, that'd be great.

[Sam does the introductions, gets a beer from the kitchen, and hands it to Shawn]

Shawn: Do you remember the last time I was here?

Sam: How could I forget!

Shawn: Go ahead. Tell everybody about it.

Sam: OK, if you insist. Well one night about two weeks ago Shawn came by. About two minutes after I let him in there was a second knock on the door, very loud.

Shawn: Yeah, I had an idea who it was. I whispered to Sam not to tell them I was here and hid behind the couch.

Sam: I went to the door. It was the police. And they asked me if anyone had come into my apartment in the last few minutes. I remembered that I gulped and told them that no one had. They accepted this and went away. As I was closing my front door I asked myself: What have I done? I had just lied to the police, and I felt very funny.

Zainab: Did you feel that you had done something wrong?

Sam: I don't know what I felt. I felt . . . well, funny. I was agitated, of course, but also a little confused. I didn't feel that what I had done was right, but I didn't feel that it was wrong either. The morality of my action was . . . up in the air, undefined.

Shawn: Hey, man, *I* think you did what was right.

Jerry: Sam, do you mean that the morality of what you did was unclear to you or that there was no settled morality?

Sam: The second.

Zainab: That is precisely what a subjectivist should say, to be consistent. Since Sam had no moral feelings one way or the other about what he did, so far what he did was neither right nor wrong.

Jerry: I don't think we are quite through thinking about subjectivism.

Maria: I think that you are right, Jerry, but I have a problem with cultural moral relativism that I really would like to talk about. The basic idea of cultural moral relativism is that our culture determines what is right and wrong for us. Here is my problem: What happens if you are a member of more than one society? In my village in Mexico, where I lived as a little girl, it would have been out of the question for me, as a young woman, to go on a date with a young man, just the two of us. My mother would not have allowed it. Whenever a young woman went out, she always had *una chaperona*, a chaperone. Even here in America my mother and my grandmother disapprove of my going out alone on a date. In many ways I think of my culture as my Mexican heritage, but when it comes to dating I prefer the freer American way. I see myself as having two cultures. So which culture determines what is right for me, according to cultural moral relativism?

Shawn: You guys go ahead. I'll be a fly on the wall.

Jerry: Thanks, Shawn. Since our last conversation I have done some reading about cultural moral relativism. Back in the early twentieth century Herskovits and other anthropologists investigated traditional cultures that were fairly tightly circumscribed. For traditional cultures, like the cultures in Africa where Herskovits did a lot of his fieldwork, there was no question about what culture a man or woman belonged to. It's different with our multicultural society here in America. Here one can belong to more than one culture. Here in American there is a mainstream, dominant culture, but there are also Mexican, Korean, Native American, and other cultural strains, each of which amounts to a distinctive constituent culture within American society; and many Americans, like Maria, belong to the mainstream culture and also to one of the other constituent cultures. What Maria's example shows us is that cultural moral relativism cannot be followed by a person who belongs to more than one culture.

Sarah: Why not?

Jerry: Well, if you belong to two cultures and one of your cultures tells you that doing something—going out on a date without a chaperone, say—is morally allowable and the other tells you it is wrong, you can't follow the rule "do what your culture says."

Sarah: So you have to decide which culture you will follow. Where is the problem?

Vishnu: If I may, the problem is this: cultural moral relativism can provide no basis on which to decide which culture to follow. It cannot tell us to follow the culture that directs us to the right action. This would concede that there is some test or standard for moral rightness over and above what cultures say. Herskovits himself was clear on this point as it relates to human rights. If human beings have rights simply by virtue of being human persons, then there is a moral standard that applies across cultures and exists independently of what cultures say. In 1947 Herskovits on behalf of the American Anthropological Association Executive Board wrote a statement objecting to the United Nations Universal Declaration of Human Rights. Herskovits was being perfectly consistent. If cultural moral relativism is correct, cultures determine their own morality, and there are no transcultural human rights, or any other transcultural moral standard.

Sarah: So anthropology rejects human rights, like our right to say what we think and not to be tortured?

Vishnu: No, not every anthropologist accepts cultural moral relativism and rejects human rights. More recently some anthropologists have questioned cultural moral relativism by giving weight to human rights. Some anthropologists, for instance, have been concerned that the practice of female circumcision—the practice that Zainab mentioned last time—which is followed by several cultural groups, may violate the individual human rights of the women and girls affected.

Sam: Where do these human rights come from? I feel that it is right to let people express their opinions and that it is wrong to use torture, but I guess I am like Herskovits in being very doubtful about human rights.

Vishnu: Herskovits was more than doubtful. He had to deny there was any such thing. And you do too, as long as you accept subjectivism. Human rights would constitute a test for the correctness of personal moral feelings just as much as they constitute a test for the correctness of cultural moral beliefs.

Sam: OK, I think I see that. I repeat: Where do these human rights you are talking about come from?

Vishnu: I have to concede that for some there is an issue about the status and even the existence of human rights.

Jerry: But wait! Didn't the founders of our country speak of our inalienable rights? The Declaration of Independence proclaims that we have the right to life and to liberty and the pursuit of happiness.

Vishnu: Yes, and a few years later at the time of the French Revolution a French assembly drafted The Declaration of the Rights of Man, proclaiming that men are born free and equal in rights. So much is historical fact. Several have noted, however, that before the eighteenth century there was no mention of general human rights. And some around the world have seen human rights as a Western or Euro-American invention.

Sam: Well, there it is. The idea of human rights was invented in the 1700s, and before that time they did not exist.

Jerry: Not so fast. We can't conclude that human rights did not exist before they were given a name. Would you reason that viral disease didn't exist before viruses were discovered and named?

Vishnu: The issue about human rights might be put this way: Were they invented, so that they came into existence merely as concepts; or were they recognized as something human beings do have and have always had? And of course there are further questions about just what rights there are. The right to liberty is one thing. The right to the enjoyment of leisure may be another.

Yusuf: Also, if we agree that there is a right to liberty, there may still be a question about what respecting that right requires. Could it take different forms in different cultures? Of course the question about the form or requirements of a human right, and whether its proper observance might vary from place to place, is different from the question whether human beings do have human rights. It could be that human beings have basic human rights and the proper observance of them varies from one part of the world to another. In any case in its own Universal Declaration of Human Rights the United Nations said that it was *recognizing* human rights.

Zainab: I for one am very clear that there are human rights and that the practice Vishnu referred to violates women's human rights. Vishnu called it "female circumcision," but that is a misleading euphemism. Often the surgery involves cutting away most or all of the external sex organs and sewing shut the vagina. This terrible operation is better known as "female genital mutilation" because that is what it is—mutilation—and it violates a woman's right to bodily integrity. My mother and I have long opposed female genital mutilation. For years my mother has been active in Women for Human Rights, which has tried to raise the consciousness of people, especially men, in countries where this demeaning practice is followed.

Maria: You are Muslim, aren't you, and isn't this something that is done to girls as a part of your religion?

Zainab: Yes, I am Muslim, but female genital mutilation is not a Muslim practice. In many Muslim countries it does not occur. In my native country, Iran, it is not practiced. This terrible custom is not religious, it is cultural. Although it is found in some Muslim societies, it is most prevalent in non-Muslim societies in Africa, and it is in African countries that my mother's organization does most of its work in cooperation with African women's groups.

Jerry: Zainab has put her finger on a real problem for cultural moral relativism. Let me try to formulate the problem as I see it. Cultural moral relativism is consistent with anthropologists observing and comparing, as to difference and similarity, the moral beliefs of different cultures. They can observe that head-hunting is allowed in one culture and not allowed in another. But if cultural moral relativism is right, then there should be no meaningful comparisons of the moral beliefs of different cultures *as to which is better*. According to cultural moral relativism, we can't make such comparisons because they presuppose what cultural moral relativism says does not exist, namely, a transcultural moral standard *above what cultures say is right or wrong*—a higher standard—by which we can judge such cultural moral beliefs. But clearly we can and do make such comparisons. What Zainab is saying implies that the cultural belief that female genital mutilation is wrong is a better moral belief than the cultural belief that female genital mutilation is morally allowable. We have here an argument that shows cultural moral relativism is wrong.

Zainab: Yes, I would say that. And I think that cultural moral relativism has related problems too. For one thing cultural moral relativism has to deny that there can be moral progress in a society's moral beliefs. Cultural moral relativism can allow that the moral beliefs of a society might *change* over time, but it cannot allow that such a change would be a *change for the better*. If a cultural moral relativist went to a New Guinea or upper Amazon society at one time and found that they believed headhunting was morally allowed, even required, and then returned at a later time and found that those in the society had come to believe that it was not morally allowable, he or she, as a cultural moral relativist, could recognize this as a change in that society's moral belief. But he or she could not recognize it as progress, as change for the better in that society's moral belief. He or she couldn't because recognizing it as progress would involve an implicit appeal to a higher standard, a standard above cultural moral beliefs, by which that society's moral beliefs could be judged. Counter to cultural moral relativism, it is evident that there have been changes for the better in the moral beliefs of some societies. So here is another argument against cultural moral relativism.

Sam: Are we really sure that this change in the moral beliefs of the headhunting society *is* progress?

Zainab: I am sure. However, even if I am wrong, it is at least a meaningful judgment that this change in cultural moral belief is a change for the better, and even its being a meaningful judgment is ruled out by cultural moral relativism. For just its being a meaningful judgment requires a higher standard than the moral beliefs themselves. And if you are looking for other judgments that are more clearly true, they abound. Take the judgment that a change from the moral belief that female genital mutilation is allowable to the moral belief that it is wrong is progress. Or, to use an American example, the change from the moral belief that it is all right to pay women less for the same work that men do to the moral belief that it is not all right. And I could give you more examples.

Jerry: The problem here for cultural moral relativism is like the comparison problem that I identified, but here it involves comparing the moral beliefs of a single culture or society over time and making the judgment that its moral beliefs have changed for the better. Since cultural moral relativism has to deny a higher standard by which any society's moral beliefs can be evaluated it has both these problems, and it opens itself to both my and Zainab's arguments.

Zainab: And while we are at it, we might mention one more problem for cultural moral relativism, which again forms the basis of an argument against it. It is related to the others in that it too turns on the fact that cultural moral relativism has to deny a higher, cross-cultural or transcultural standard. But it is slightly different. If cultural moral relativism were a true view of the nature of morality, then there should be no questions that members of a society could raise about the correctness of their society's moral beliefs. This would mean that if you lived in a society in which, say, slavery was said to be right, like the society of the southern United States in the nineteenth century, there would be no question about the correctness of that belief. Once a nineteenth-century southerner in America saw that his or her culture approved of owning slaves, he or she should conclude that of course it is all right. Obviously people, like many who lived in the American south in the nineteenth century, do have questions about some of their society's moral beliefs. They may even have the strong sense that their culture is wrong.

Vishnu: Zainab, I can see that you have thought about cultural moral relativism quite a lot.

Zainab: Yes, I guess that's true. My family left Iran when I was a little girl in great part because the culture there denied the equality of women and, against the Qur'anic teachings of Islam, denied the rights of women. Imagine how shocked I was to find in America, in some intellectual circles, the idea that morality is relative to one's culture.

Vishnu: And now you and your mother are active on behalf of women's rights, really human rights. Your efforts are similar to those of my wife, Kavita. In India, our homeland, women are for cultural reasons often given a subservient role. It is true that we have had a woman prime minister in India, and more and more women are entering the professions in India. Still, overall, especially outside the cities, women have a difficult life. In the past in India, sati was an accepted practice. When sati, otherwise known as widow burning or widow immolation, is followed a widow burns herself alive by having herself put onto her dead husband's funeral pyre. Although sati is now against the law, and has been for more than a century, every now and then there is an occurrence of this terrible practice. In Hinduism, the main religious tradition of India, or, rather, in one of Hinduism's cultural manifestations, often widows are regarded as "inauspicious." Very often they are shunned and not allowed to participate in family life. It is the plight of widows, and in general the status of women in Indian culture, that Kavita is working with others to change. Their main weapon is education, and Kavita is active is getting funding for this educational effort.

Maria: I have some sympathy for following one's own tradition. It is clear, though, that not every traditional custom should be followed. There is a place in this world for reformers.

Jerry: There sure is, Maria. The world, or America anyway, is a better place because we have had reformers like Susan B. Anthony and Martin Luther King, Jr. And if cultural moral relativism were a right view of morality, there would be no place for reformers.

Sam: I agree that reformers have made a real contribution, but I don't see what reforming the law has to do with cultural moral relativism. Jerry pointed out last time that subjectivism is not a thesis about what is legal and illegal. The same can be said for cultural moral relativism. So both views can allow that there are reformers.

Jerry: You are right, Sam, that the existence of legal reformers would present no problem for either view. But often reformers seek to reform social attitudes. Susan B. Anthony worked for an amendment to the United States Constitution that would give women the vote, but she did so by trying to change the popular attitude in America about women voting. The same can be said of Martin Luther King, Jr. Yes, he and others in the civil rights movement sought to change discriminatory laws, but more important King worked to change discriminatory social attitudes that approved of treating black Americans as second-class citizens. Both of these reformers were *moral* reformers who were trying to change the moral beliefs of their society for the better.

Maria: So, for the same reason that cultural moral relativism would not and could not allow that there is such a thing as progress in the moral beliefs of a society, it cannot allow that there could be a moral reformer.

Jerry: Yes that's it.

Sarah: Of course the arguments that Jerry and Zainab have given us assume that there is a "higher standard" by which the beliefs or moral codes of different cultures can be judged.

Jerry: True. But there is, isn't there? If you say there isn't then you have to allow that if some society morally approves of some action then that action is as right as any action can be. And it doesn't matter what that action is. It could be female genital mutilation, slavery, child prostitution, anti-Semitism, the persecution of some minority group, or anything else. Are you happy with this?

Sarah: I will have to think about it.

3

⁓✥⁓

More on "Higher Standards," Arguments against Subjectivism, Why Maria is not a Cultural Moral Relativist, and Manners versus Morality

SETTING: Sam's apartment a few days later. All except Shawn are present.

Vishnu: There is something I think we should clarify. Remember how last time we were talking about a "higher standard," by which the moral beliefs or moral codes of a culture could be evaluated. Such a higher standard would be above the moral beliefs of a culture and provide a basis for judging their correctness. That means that if there were such a higher standard, cultural moral relativism cannot be right; and if cultural moral relativism is right, there can't be such a higher standard. This much we were clear on last time. But there is a point to clarify here, something I reflected on after our conversation last time. That "higher standard" doesn't have to be a single unvarying standard that in each and every instance determines what is morally right.

Jerry: Why doesn't it? It seems to me that last time the arguments that Zainab and I presented showed pretty conclusively that there is such an absolute higher standard.

Vishnu: Yes, I agree that we could come away from our previous conversation with that impression. But, I don't think we have to accept that there is one and only one higher standard in this absolute sense, at least not based on our reasoning last time. Here is why. What we saw last time is that if we can compare the moral codes of different cultures as to which is better, or judge that the moral beliefs of our own culture or society have gotten better, more enlightened, or just examine the moral beliefs of our own society and judge that morally they should not be followed, then we are in some way appealing to some standard higher than these cultural moral beliefs themselves. I am not challenging this implication. I think that it is right. But saying this much does not mean that the standard appealed to in making these judgments absolutely has to be the same in each instance. What is appealed to just has to be a moral consideration other than cultural beliefs, which provides grounds for saying one cultural moral belief is better than another. For instance, it could be human rights. And I think this is the standard that Zainab and I were appealing to last time. But in other cases it could be the good effects of what we do, the general welfare of society, the fair and equal treatment of all members of the society, or having decent respect for each member of society.

Each of these is an identifiable moral consideration, and each is independent of the moral beliefs of a society. Herskovits saw this independence regarding human rights, but the same thing holds for the other considerations. All that is necessary for our previous arguments is that some of these independent moral considerations should operate as a "higher standard." There doesn't have to be only one higher standard.

Sam: I guess that we can accept your clarification, Vishnu. Even with it, going back to those arguments that Jerry and Zainab gave us last time—the lack-of-comparison and no-possible-progress arguments, to name two—I think we can see that subjectivism doesn't have these problems. A subjectivist can easily compare the moral codes of two societies and say one is better, and he or she can easily regard a change in his or her society's moral beliefs as progress. A subjectivist can do so because he or she has a higher standard than the moral beliefs of his or her society, one that is independent of his or her society's moral beliefs. Namely, his or her own moral feelings. Let's say I live in a society that regards it wrong to provide marijuana to those who need it to alleviate pain. I feel it is right to do so. Then my society changes its collective mind and comes to agree with me. This is moral progress for my society, I could and would say as a subjectivist, even if the cultural moral relativist could never admit it.

Jerry: Maybe subjectivism doesn't have precisely the problems that cultural moral relativism has, but it has its own version of these problems. Take the lack-of-comparison problem. As it applies to cultural moral relativism, it relates to a lack of comparison of the moral beliefs of two cultures or societies as to which is better. In the version that applies to subjectivism, it relates to a lack of comparison of the moral beliefs or feelings of two individuals as to which is better. Say that I feel that it is wrong to provide marijuana to those who need it to alleviate pain, like most of the individuals in the society you imagined. You feel it is right to provide marijuana in these cases. On what basis would you say that your moral belief is better? It can't be the bare fact that *you* have this belief or this feeling. For I could argue the same way, citing *my* moral feeling.

Sam: I would still say that my own moral feelings are morally important *to me.*

Zainab: Yes, you could, Sam. And I would say that moral feeling and even conviction are exceedingly important. I am really put off by people who are lukewarm about important moral issues. But it is even more important to have the *right* moral feelings. I liked your example about providing marijuana for patients for medical purposes. I think that your moral feelings were exactly right. And I think that there is a reason why they are right, but not one that you as a committed subjectivist will like. Let's say you started out feeling that it was wrong to provide marijuana to those who need it to alleviate pain. Then you change your moral belief or feeling—belief and feeling come to the same thing here. So now you come to believe or feel that it is right. Is this just a change in your moral belief, or is it a change for the better, so that it is progress in your moral beliefs? I think it would be progress. If it is, though, it can't be because of what you believe or feel because both the first and second are your beliefs. I suppose you could say that your second belief is better just because it is the one you have now. But then if you changed back to your first belief for some reason, you'd have to say that *that* change was progress too, which would be funny. The reason I think that your second belief or feeling—the one you said you actually had, the belief or feeling that it is right to provide marijuana to those who need it to alleviate pain—is the right one is that it is supported by a relevant objective reason. The providing of medicinal marijuana is right because it reflects a decent respect for individuals and their needs. This is one of the independent moral considerations that Vishnu mentioned. He presented it as a moral consideration that exists independently of a society's moral beliefs, but it is equally a consideration that exists independently of individuals' moral beliefs or feelings. Your moral feeling was right because it was *rightly formed*, resting on the basis of a respect for persons and their needs.

Jerry: It seems that both cultural moral relativism and subjectivism have their problems. If moral rightness and wrongness can rest on these moral considerations, which are independent of what societies say and of what individuals feel or believe, then it is beginning to look as though morality is *objective*, just as I said.

Maria: There is something that is not clear to me. Sometimes I follow the ways of my Mexican upbringing and sometimes I follow the ways of my American culture—I mean the mainstream and dominant American culture. I follow my Mexican heritage more in showing actually *showing*, respect for the elders in my family, and when I go out with my friends I follow the American way and go out without a chaperone. Am I then a cultural moral relativist, but one with cultural schizophrenia?

Zainab: No, I don't think so, Maria. I suspect that you are not a cultural moral relativist at all. It is not acting in accord with your culture, or in your case one or the other of them, that makes a person a cultural moral relativist. One could follow nearly all, or even all, of the moral beliefs or customs of one's culture and still not be a cultural moral relativist. In my behavior I follow much of my Iranian culture, but I reject cultural moral relativism. I do because I am prepared to question the moral credentials of at least some of my Iranian culture's moral beliefs. Like you I too participate in and have two cultures. In the same way that I sometimes question my Iranian heritage, I am prepared to question some of the moral beliefs of my American culture.

Vishnu: Zainab brings out an important point. Let's say that you had only one culture and that you always acted in accord with the moral beliefs of your one culture. Still you might not be a cultural moral relativist. As Zainab said, it is not acting in accord with one's culture's moral beliefs that defines a person as a cultural moral relativist, similarly acting in accord with one's own moral feelings does not in itself make one a subjectivist. There are several reasons why this is so. Zainab pointed to one of them: you can follow your culture's moral beliefs, but be prepared to question their validity—something a consistent cultural moral relativist cannot do. There are other reasons why someone who follows the moral beliefs of her society is not necessarily a cultural moral relativist. Maria, you said that you followed your Mexican culture's ways in showing respect for your elders. Let me ask you why you follow the way of your Mexican culture here and not the way of the more mainstream American culture?

Maria: If I spoke to my mother the way some of my friends who are not Latina speak to their mothers, my mother would be shocked. She would be deeply hurt.

Vishnu: I understand. Here is another reason why simply following the moral belief of your culture does not make you a cultural moral relativist. You have a moral reason for following the moral custom of your culture—not doing so would deeply hurt your mother. A cultural moral relativist would not need any such reason. In fact a cultural moral relativist would deny that there could be a moral reason for following the moral beliefs of his culture. Once his culture says it is right to do something, that makes it right. Any justification in terms of the kind of moral reason that you gave constitutes an appeal to the kind of "higher standard"—one of them—that cultural moral relativism has to deny.

Sarah: After our last conversation I went home and thought about all that cultural moral relativism would have to say is morally right, and, OK, I can see that cultural moral relativism has a problem in light of the fact that some cultures have approved of such terrible things as slavery and the persecution of minorities. But cultural moral relativism is right on some things. I think that it could be right about good manners. Good manners are relative to a culture or society. Whether it is acceptable to eat with your fingers or eating with silverware is appropriate, how close you stand to someone in conversation, what clothes are appropriate when you go out in public, are all covered by good manners and are decided by the culture one is in. It seems that societies determine what will be good manners, and a society's determination of good manners holds for that society—just as cultural moral relativism says about moral rightness, except that it should have limited itself to manners, as opposed to moral rightness.

Vishnu: I think that there is something to your point, Sarah. Cultures or societies could well determine what will be good manners, even if they don't determine morality. And your point brings it out how, although both relate to proper or acceptable behavior, there is a difference between morally right action and observance of good manners. I remember a time I was at table with some colleagues and various dignitaries at Cambridge. As I recall, a retiring professor was being honored. It was a formal dinner and there were several courses. When the fish course was served I made the blunder of using the wrong fork. After a few bites I realized I wasn't using the fish fork, and I recall that I was embarrassed. But I didn't feel I had done anything *morally* wrong.

Jerry: I know that some think there is a big difference between manners or good manners and morally right actions, and often there is, as in Vishnu's example, but sometimes violating good manners can amount to a moral transgression. Manners and morality are not two utterly separate spheres.

Zainab: Maybe I can provide an example to support what Jerry says. Sarah said that appropriate dress is a matter of good manners. I think that we might accept that, although in the background there may be a religious influence. There certainly is a religious influence in Muslim countries, where wearing hijab is required. Islam requires both men and women to dress modestly, although the requirement of modesty is most evident in the clothing for women. The precise clothing required for women is not specified in the Qur'an, and the dress regarded as hijab can vary a lot from one culture to another in the Muslim world. In Afghanistan many women wear a burka, which covers the entire body, including hands and feet; even the face is covered by a kind of mesh mask. Around the Persian Gulf women often wear an abaya; usually black, it covers the head to the forehead and drapes the rest of the body. In Iran a chador is worn. Very often Muslim women wear a khimar, or head scarf, which covers the head except for the face and comes down to the waist. That is what I am wearing. So what qualifies as wearing hijab varies with the culture. It is a matter of manners, it may be said. Now let's say that a non-Muslim American woman went to Saudi Arabia and walked around with no head covering and bare arms. For one thing this would get her into trouble with the religious police. Forget about that. What I want to draw to your attention is that this violation of good manners would also be deeply offensive to her hosts in that country and in this way would take on a moral significance.

Andrew: Let me provide another example. I have lived in this country for several years now, going to university. For the first eighteen years of my life

I lived in West Africa. I grew up in Nigeria. There it is considered impolite to use your left hand. You always hand things to other people with your right hand. My father, who has lived his whole life in Nigeria, would be deeply offended if someone handed him something with his left hand. When I came to this country I used to winch when someone would hand me a book with his left hand. But I finally got used to it.

Jerry: Good examples of how manners sometimes become moral matters. Not always, but sometimes when you violate good manners you offend people and then it is more than bad manners.

Vishnu: Maybe violations of good manners take on a moral significance precisely when they offend, or deeply offend, someone; and it is giving offense, not violating good manners *in itself* that is morally wrong.

Jerry: I think that there may be more to the connection between good manners and morality than that. Let's allow that what counts as good manners is set by a society or culture, as Sarah suggests. Couldn't there be times when by observing good manners we would be doing what is morally wrong?

Sarah: Do you have an example in mind?

Jerry: Say there is a society in which when you came to dinner it was good manners to present your host with a small gem. These gems are not exceedingly expensive and are available from gem merchants. The gem merchants get their gems from suppliers, and the suppliers use child laborers to harvest the gems. These children are indentured workers who invariably come from the poorest families, and the suppliers buy their labor by paying their parents a certain amount of money. Although the amount of money is not great, the children have to work for years to pay back that amount, in order to earn their freedom. During these years they get no education and live under the worst conditions. Many die in their servitude. Now if I observe the good manners of this society I contribute to this evil practice, and surely that is wrong. I'd bring flowers instead.

Sarah: Is this an example taken from an existing society?

Jerry: No, my case is made-up. But it is realistic enough. The point is that in such a case it would be wrong to follow "good manners."

Vishnu: Your case shows us that there may at times be a tighter connection between manners and morality than I, for one, had thought. Strictly you are not denying that societies determine good manners. It is just that at times in violating good manners we can do what is morally wrong and, allowing your hypothetical case, at times we may do what is morally wrong in observing good manners.

Sarah: So, even if societies determine good manners, it is not that they determine good manners *as opposed to* what is morally right, as I suggested, for violating and observing good manners may have moral significance.

Jerry: Yes that's it.

Vishnu: This discussion brings up another issue for cultural moral relativism. Let me go back to Andrew's example. In Nigeria, people would be deeply offended if someone handed them something with his left hand. Then, you said, Andrew, when you came to America you got used to it, and finally there was no longer anything offensive about it. Andrew's story raises another question about cultural moral relativism and what it says about the determination—not of manners—but of moral rightness. Say that someone moves from the culture of his birth to a new culture, as you did. Which culture determines what is right for him, the culture in which he grew up or the culture to which he moves and in which he now lives? And if there is a switch, when does it occur? Last time Maria raised a question about which culture should be followed when one has *two* cultures. Here the question is similar. Which culture, according to cultural moral relativism, is one's single morality-defining culture, the culture one grew up in or the culture one moves to?

Sarah: When in Rome do as the Romans do.

Zainab: Even if it is female genital mutilation? If I moved to an East African country, I wouldn't suddenly come to feel it is all right, let alone an obligation, to circumcise my daughter.

Sarah: I see your point. And I see that I can't say on behalf of cultural moral relativism that it is all right to do as the Romans do when in Rome unless the Romans are doing what is morally wrong. I can't for the reason Vishnu gave last time. My saying such a thing would allow that Roman culture could be approving of what is wrong, and that postulates a higher moral standard above what a culture approves of.

Vishnu: Exactly right.

4

~∞~

Tolerance, Conscience, Moral Universals, Ethnocentrism, and Moral Absolutes

SETTING: Sam's apartment a week later. Everyone except Shawn is present.

Sarah: I have been thinking about why cultural moral relativism seems right to me. One reason is that when all is said and done it is a tolerant view of other cultures. It is nonjudgmental.

Jerry: But is this tolerance always a good thing? Remember that some societies or cultures have approved of terrible things, including anti-Semitism, slavery, and child prostitution. But there is another problem for cultural moral relativism regarding tolerance, an internal problem. What does the cultural moral relativist regard as the *scope* of this value? If the cultural moral relativist says it is a value for everyone, then he is putting forward a transcultural value, which his own theory says does not exist.

Sarah: I still think that tolerance is valuable.

Jerry: So do I. It is morally right to be tolerant, except of evil practices. I am not saying tolerance is not a moral value. I am only saying that when we recognize it as a moral value for everyone, we stop being cultural moral relativists.

Sam: In the same way, I can see, subjectivism could not put forward tolerance as a moral value for everyone. Still it seems to *embody* a tolerance for other persons' moral feelings, for what each person's individual conscience tells that person. I have been rethinking subjectivism and why it seems right to me. Isn't it just saying follow your own conscience?

Jerry: If that is all it is saying, then it allows for an objective right and wrong. For when you follow your conscience you follow what you *know* is right and wrong independently of your moral feelings. Your conscience tells you that if you violate some moral principle you accept, then you will be guilty of wrongdoing. So, for instance, if you keep the money in a wallet you find on the sidewalk, your conscience tells you that you will be guilty of stealing. And that principle exists independently of what you feel. It exists even if you somehow convince yourself to feel it would be all right to keep the money you found—although, Sam, I know that *you* would never feel it was all right to keep the money.

Vishnu: Jerry, I think that you have given us one meaning of "conscience." For that meaning, when we act against our conscience we act against objective moral rules or principles that we have internalized—principles that do not depend on what people say or believe or feel. This is certainly a coherent conception of the conscience, and of course, it is at odds with a relativistic account of morality. There are, however, other ways of understanding the conscience. For instance, a cultural moral relativist could understand it as an internalization of the moral customs or rules of a person's culture or society. Again, a subjectivist could understand a person's conscience as reminding her or him of what she or he feels is right and feels is wrong. In both of these relativistic constructions no objective right and wrong is presupposed. And, using the last subjectivist meaning, as Sam says, subjectivism could be saying, "follow your conscience."

Jerry: Surely the first meaning, the meaning I gave, is the primary meaning. If you do not act in accord with your conscience, you do what is wrong.

Sam: That is also true with the subjectivist meaning of conscience. If I act against my conscience in the sense of my moral feelings, then I do what is wrong. And this is just what subjectivism says.

Sarah: Can we restate subjectivism as "if a person does what she feels is wrong, then she does what is wrong"?

Vishnu: Well no, we can't, not if we mean by "subjectivism" what we have been talking about since our first conversation a couple of weeks ago. Subjectivism, as we understood it then, says, first, that what the individual feels is right or wrong makes what he does right or wrong and, second, the individual's feelings make it right or wrong for him or her, but not for others. This "standard subjectivism" implies that if I act against my own moral feelings, and against my conscience in this sense, then I will be doing what is wrong. But subjectivism says more than this, as I have just reminded everyone. Moreover, one does not have to be a subjectivist to accept the moral principle that if a person does what she or he feels is wrong, then that person does what is wrong.

Sam: Really! Can you explain how someone who is not a subjectivist could accept this principle?

Vishnu: I think so. The moral principle says that a person does what is wrong if she or he does what she feels is wrong. It does not say that what *makes* the action wrong in the first place is the individual's feeling it is wrong, as subjectivism does. The principle allows that what makes the action wrong, if it is, is an objective moral consideration distinct from the individual's moral feelings. Once a person comes to feel that an action is wrong, whether it is or not, then if she or he goes ahead and does it, she or he goes against her or his own moral convictions. And it is this going against one's convictions that makes doing the action wrong, according to the principle.

Jerry: So, as far as this principle is concerned, it does not matter if the contemplated action is right or wrong. If you *feel* it is wrong, it is wrong for you to do it.

Vishnu: Yes,that's it.

Jerry: Then it allows what Zainab argued last time, namely, that moral feelings can be wrong or they can be right.

Vishnu: That's right, and so clearly it can be accepted by one who is not a subjectivist.

Jerry: Let's say that I feel that it is right to do something that is in fact wrong. Won't I be in a position in which I cannot avoid doing what is wrong? Let me construct an imaginary case. Imagine a young man, a German in Nazi Germany at the time of World War II, a contemporary of Sartre and his student, except that he is in Germany, not France. Let's imagine that this young man is a member of the Hitler Youth and has acquired the Nazi attitudes instilled into its members. His parents, though, are trying to help their Jewish friends by getting them false papers so that they can leave Germany. Being indoctrinated, this young man feels that it would be right for him to denounce his parents. In fact, as we can all see, his denouncing his parents to the Nazi police would be wrong. For one thing, they are his own parents. For another there would be terrible consequences for them in Nazi detention, and also the aid they were giving their Jewish friends in helping them to escape from Germany will be cut off. In the light of the principle, then, he acts wrongfully if he does not denounce his parents; but also he would be doing what is wrong, as we all appreciate, if he does denounce them.

Vishnu: Yes that is an implication. Maybe it is not so odd. Maybe your young man was responsible for letting himself be indoctrinated. Maybe he should have questioned what the members of the Hitler Youth wanted him to believe. And, in any case, one of the wrong actions may be much worse morally than the other. In relation to subjectivism the thing to notice here is that if your young man acts in accord with his moral feelings, in the case as you have presented it, he will be doing what is wrong. And this too a subjectivist cannot accept.

Sam: I notice that this case, along with Jerry's claim that we will all recognize as wrong the young man's denunciation of his parents, appeals to a "higher standard" than personal feelings. I must confess I am sympathetic to what Jerry says about the wrongness of his following his moral feelings in this case, and not only because I happen to be Jewish.

Maria: There is another way to understand what our conscience is. We can understand it as an infallible inner guide to right action. If your conscience says that what you are about to do, or are told to do, is right, then it is right; and if your conscience says it is wrong, then it is wrong.

Vishnu: This is yet another way of understanding what the conscience is. But it does raise some questions. Let us say that I feel doing something is right, does that mean that my conscience approves of it?

Maria: No, it doesn't. The young man in Jerry's example felt that it was right to denounce his parents, but that was not his conscience speaking. Those were only his deluded moral feelings.

Jerry: For this understanding of the conscience, then, we can always ask when we feel that something is right or wrong: "Is this my conscience speaking, or are these moral feelings I have misguided?"

Maria: Well, maybe sometimes we would have that question. But of course we have tests in those cases. We have those "higher standards" we have talked about, and they are objective.

Jerry: So our conscience is an infallible guide to moral rightness, but our judgment that it is our conscience speaking is fallible. Still this much is clear: on the understanding of the conscience proposed by Maria it is a guide to a moral rightness and wrongness that exists *before* we have moral feelings one way or the other, which I am happy to admit, but subjectivism cannot admit.

Sarah: It looks as though cultural moral relativism is in a stronger position here. A cultural moral relativist can agree that our conscience is a guide to a moral rightness that exists prior to our moral feelings. He or she can say, as Vishnu pointed out, that our conscience is formed by our society and tells us what our society counts as right and wrong.

Vishnu: So there are several ways to understand what "the conscience" means. It is open to Sam to understand it in a subjectivist way, and it is open to a cultural moral relativist to understand it in accord with cultural moral relativism. Also it is open to Jerry to understand it in his objectivist way, just as it is open to Maria to understand the conscience as an infallible moral guide.

Jerry: Yes, it is open to a subjectivist and a cultural moral relativist to understand what "the conscience" means in their respective ways. However, we should not forget all the problems for cultural moral relativism that Zainab and I have raised, which, we saw, also relate to subjectivism when they are slightly refocused. And if the arguments that these problems engender refute subjectivism and cultural moral relativism, they also refute their ways of understanding the conscience.

Vishnu: So, regarding the correctness of subjectivism and cultural moral relativism, much depends on the conclusiveness of the arguments that Jerry and Zainab presented the second time we met. And there is something else we should consider in thinking about cultural moral relativism. Sometimes the point is made by cultural relativists that the values set up by a cultural group have a functional value. They are valuable in perpetuating the group. Herskovits said that there are several ways the primary family might be constituted in a society. There might be one husband and one wife or one husband and several wives or one wife and several husbands. These arrangements, he said, could be evaluated in terms of their functional value, according to whether they perpetuated the group. The family arrangement in Dahomey, where the family unit consisted of one husband and several wives, he judged, had this functional value.

Sam: Doesn't this set up a standard higher than cultural ways by which they can be tested?

Vishnu: It certainly seems to. And if the functional test can be applied to cultural beliefs about family arrangements, presumably it could be applied in evaluating other cultural moral beliefs.

Jerry: It seems that Herskovits was inconsistent.

Vishnu: Maybe, but maybe not. He would be inconsistent if he thought that the functional test was a test of moral rightness. Then it would amount to a "higher standard" than cultural moral beliefs. But, while he thought that cultural ways could be evaluated, apparently he understood the functional test as a means of evaluating the *effectiveness* of cultural ways, not their moral rightness. If cultural ways contributed to the survival and viability of the culture, then they were effective.

Zainab: So, for cultural moral relativism, if a culture or society holds that, say, head-hunting is right then it is right for that society and if that cultural belief or practice functions to help the society survive it is furthermore "effective." Clearly a society's moral belief could be effective and at the same time be morally wrong. Some societies have allowed kidnapping and making slaves of those in other societies. And in the past other powerful societies have colonized and exploited less powerful societies, as the Europeans did in the fifteenth and later centuries. These more powerful societies followed effective societal beliefs, since doing so led to the flourishing of these societies, but the practices they followed were immoral.

Vishnu: Some might argue with you about the morality of colonization. Some good things may have come from the British Raj, the time of the British rule in India. But it would be hard to argue with your main point.

Jerry: So, finally, cultural moral relativism has no grounds on which to reject immoral cultural beliefs; just as subjectivism has no grounds on which to reject any individual's immoral feelings. If either one were correct there would be no universal moral values.

Yusuf: When all is said and done, though, it seems to me that there are moral universals that hold from one culture to the next. I cannot imagine any culture that would condone murder or not caring for your family.

Andrew: Yes and sometimes the differences in values between cultures that we think we see do not really exist. We think they exist because we look at the ways of other cultures ethnocentrically, that is, through the lens of our own culture. If my father came here, to America, and somebody handed him something with his left hand, my father might think that he was either trying to offend him or was utterly lacking in good manners. Really, it would be neither. Here is another example. Paul, a friend of mine, is from West Africa. Like me, he is attending an American university. In the first weeks that he was here he found himself with a question. He wondered why students on his campus started to greet him as they approached him on the main campus walkway, but then would not speak as they passed. They at first seemed friendly and then quickly changed and became mean and unfriendly. Was it something he was doing, he wondered? Paul came from a community in Cameroon in which when you walk down the street you greet everyone with at least an *Ashia,* a Cameroonian term of friendly greeting, and everyone greets you. Nothing less is required by basic civility. In America it is different. Often people on a busy street pass one another with no acknowledgment at all. A smile in passing someone on a street might be more than friendly. In fact the American students on Paul's campus were being more than friendly, but Paul saw their reactions in the light of his own culture and he thought they were being unfriendly. In time he learned, and now looking back on it he laughs about his misunderstanding.

Vishnu: I think that Andrew's point about ethnocentrically viewing cultures other than our own is important. Ethnocentrism is sometimes characterized as putting one's own society at the center of things and rating other societies in reference to it or, alternatively, as taking one's own society's way of life to be preferred to all others. What it amounts to, as Andrew nicely put it, is looking at other cultures through the lens of one's own culture. Anthropologists do all they can to avoid it. In Andrew's example Paul's unconscious ethnocentrism led him to see what was really the same as what occurred in his culture as different from it—he saw an American friendly greeting as an expression of unfriendliness. Notice that it works the other way as well. Ethnocentrism can lead us to think that things done in another culture are the same as in our culture when really they are different.

Andrew: I am sure that it works that way as well. Do you have an illustrative example that you can give us, Vishnu?

Vishnu: I do. In fact I have two. One example is the mirror image of your father being offended if someone here in America handed him something with his left hand. Say that an American visiting Nigeria handed something to your father with his left hand. The American might not understand or miss entirely your father's reaction because the American might ethnocentrically regard his using his left hand as having no significance, just as it would have no significance in his or her American culture. The other example is one I remember from my anthropological studies. A Canadian explorer of the arctic regions reported that when the Inuit make a promise all it means to them is that at the moment they feel like doing the thing they are promising to do, and they will do it unless they change their minds. The Inuit, this explorer reported, do not feel committed when they make a promise, and when the time comes to keep the promise they often beg off and say they have something else to do. What I think happened is that the explorer asked an Inuit if he would accompany him on a journey across the ice and the Inuit said he would. The explorer took this to be a promise, as it would have been in his own homeland. For the Inuit, however, his saying he would accompany the explorer meant something like, "I will perhaps; I will unless I change my mind." The explorer, in short, read the Inuit's response to his request in terms of his own culture, or ethnocentrically. He read it as the same thing as a fellow countryman would mean if he said he would accompany him, namely the making of a promise, whereas the Inuit was saying something very different and not making a promise at all.

Jerry: Very interesting. I think that there are other examples of ethnocentrism that involve misinterpreting Inuit practices and might lead some mistakenly to infer that Inuit values are different from those in, say, American mainstream culture. Here is another example that I have gleaned from my reading in anthropology. In traditional Inuit culture as it was found in the past the Inuit family survived by hunting. On a hunting trip for musk ox, say, the husband did the actual hunting. However, the wife's contribution to their joint effort was essential. She dried out his mittens and boots, melted ice and boiled meat for dinner, and she had a warm igloo ready for her husband when he returned from a day of hunting. Also she stretched and prepared the skins of the animals he had killed so that they could be transported back to their home. If the husband had to do these things, his time for hunting would be much less. If a man's wife was ill or pregnant, then he would take the wife of another man on his hunting trip. This arrangement would be agreed to and understood by both husbands and both wives. It would also be understood that there would be sexual relations, in accord with the sexual practices of Inuit culture.

This was the practice in traditional Inuit culture. Things have changed over the last one hundred years as more and more Inuits have taken up residence in settlements. Let's imagine someone from the United States, from New York, visiting Greenland in the early decades of the twentieth century, or perhaps he hears a report of this practice of "wife sharing" from the acquaintance of an anthropological explorer. He thinks he knows just how to think of it. It is just the sort of thing he has secretly fantasized about, he thinks. He thinks that an American instance of this Inuit practice would occur if an aspiring employee in a New York corporation were to "lend" his wife to his boss for a weekend upstate.

But the American instance would not be the same thing as is done in the Inuit culture, and it is ethnocentrism that would lead my imagined American to think they are the same and to deny a shared underlying value of marital fidelity.

Maria: I find it really hard to imagine that this Inuit practice can be morally allowable. What is the difference between the Inuit practice and the American example of wife lending?

Jerry: Strictly, I am not arguing that the Inuit practice is morally allowable. I in fact think that it is morally allowable, but here I am only trying to show how, despite the way it appears to us from our cultural perspective, what goes on in the Inuit practice is not what would occur in the American instance that I gave. What is the difference? For one thing there is no coercion in the Inuit practice, while in the American case the wife might be subjected to pressure from her husband.

Sarah: Maybe there isn't this difference. You didn't say the wife was forced to go with her husband's boss for the weekend upstate. Your scenario leaves it open that she and her husband together planned this as something that would gain him favor with his boss and advance his career.

Jerry: There still is a difference. The marital relationship in the Inuit culture allows an exchange of wives. Sexual exclusivity is not a part of marital fidelity. Here in America, in the dominant mainstream culture, it is different. If you are married, sex with someone outside the marital relationship goes against the relationship and strains it. That's why if there were an instance of wife lending in America, all concerned—the husband, the wife, and the boss—would keep it quiet, even if the wife was not coerced and had taken part in the planning. In Inuit culture the sex is not that important; it is like having a meal with someone. There is nothing to keep secret. If my American example were actually to occur, I doubt if the boss's wife would be fully informed. The underlying difference is in what the marital relationship allows in the two cultures. The underlying difference is not in valuing marital fidelity.

Vishnu: Let me present another story of the same sort relating to ethnocentrism, again involving Inuit culture. Traditional Inuit culture in the arctic regions was a nomadic hunting culture. It was by hunting bears, seals, caribou, musk ox, and other arctic animals that Inuit families and communities survived, as Jerry said, and it was the hunting prowess of an Inuit man that established his stature and sense of worth. In old age it became difficult or impossible for a man who might have been a very good hunter to hunt at all. In old age he would feel that he had become a burden to his family, and he would find no enjoyment in life. Now in traditional Inuit cultures spirits and the spirit world were considered quite real. An aged Inuit may come to feel that it is time to pass to the distant land, the "Happy Hunting Grounds," where there are bear and caribou and he will have the vigor to enjoy the hunt again. In traditional Inuit culture old persons decided when it was time to make this passage. And when they did in some groups a party was given, where everyone was happy. In the midst of the party, perhaps with the aid of a son or favorite daughter, the old man would commit suicide by hanging himself, and so pass on to the Happy Hunting Grounds. All in the gathering would participate or at least celebrate the passage. Say that a young Inuit man helped his grandfather to hang himself. Consider the perception of an American, say, or of a European, who heard that he had done this. His question might be: Was he tired of caring for the old man? Did he stand to gain in his will?

Maria: It looks like assisted suicide.

Vishnu: Yes, it is assisted suicide.

Maria: Many in our society think that is wrong. My Church condemns it.

Jerry: While the Catholic Church condemns it, and many in our society do as well, there is in our society, in American mainstream society, an issue over the morality of assisted suicide. Some argue that it is humane in cases where the alternative is untreatable pain.

Vishnu: It is true that here in America there is a split opinion on the rightness of assisted suicide. But the current issue here in America about assisted suicide relates to assisting to commit suicide those who are terminally ill and in unrelenting pain. The decision of an aged Inuit to pass to the Happy Hunting Grounds has a very different context. It is important to keep in mind that different background beliefs prevailed in traditional Inuit society: a young Inuit helping his grandfather to depart from this life believes, as his grandfather does, that he will pass to the Happy Hunting Grounds. At death the grandfather will be in a place where he has his old vigor and there is an abundance of bear and caribou for him to hunt. That is the belief. In our cultural terms the young Inuit is doing something like a young American helping his grandfather to move from New Hampshire to Florida, where he will be warm during the winter. The Inuit elderly want to depart this life for their new life; it is their decision and their wish. Everyone is happy for the grandfather. But the issue of ethnocentrism is not the rightness of Inuit practice. It is the issue of just what is occurring. If we look at it ethnocentrically from the perspective of our own culture we will misperceive it. It is not an act of manipulative murder, as it might seem to us from our cultural perspective. Nor is it simply helping an aged person to end a life of hardship or suffering. It is helping an aged person to pass to another world where existence is easier and more rewarding. It is an act of caring for the elderly. True, we in the American mainstream culture may feel that this *form* of caring is misguided. But we should not on these grounds deny that there is an underlying value of caring for the aged.

Sarah: Jerry said that he was not *arguing* that the Inuit practice of "wife sharing" is morally allowable, but he said that he thinks it is. And Vishnu seems to allow that the Inuit practice of helping aged grandparents to commit suicide is morally acceptable, although, both allowed, we in our American culture may have a question about the morality of this form of caring. Jerry, are you saying that Inuit wife sharing is right, or morally allowable, but wife sharing is not morally allowable in American culture or mainstream American culture?

Jerry: Yes, that is what I think.

Sarah: And, Vishnu, are you saying, or at least allowing, that the Inuit practice of helping the aged to die may be right in traditional Inuit culture but wrong in our American culture?

Vishnu: Yes, that is essentially what I am saying.

Sarah: Then aren't we back to cultural moral relativism?

Vishnu: No, I would not say so. When I allow that the Inuit practice is right I am allowing that it is right in their culture *given their motives and factual beliefs.* Their motives are not in question; they were trying to care for their aged relatives. Their factual beliefs about a spirit world could be questioned as to their truth, of course. However, that they did hold these beliefs is well established. My allowing that the Inuit practice could be right in their culture is based on their motives and the factual beliefs they held. It is not based on the principle that if their culture approves of it, then it is right—which is the principle of cultural moral relativism. I believe that overcoming ethnocentrism can bring us to see that in many cases beneath a superficial difference in behavior there is a moral value shared by two cultures. In this case it is the shared value of caring for the aged.

Yusuf: I agree with Vishnu. Let me go further and observe that what all these stories illustrate is that when we set aside ethnocentrism we will discover that there are shared *universal* values found in all different cultures: being friendly, keeping a promise *if* a promise is made, not violating the requirements of the marital relationship, and caring for the aged in your family.

Vishnu: Sometimes those who have examined cultural differences point out that often the differences between cultures are over the *beliefs* they hold and not over underlying values. In the case of the Inuit practice of assisting the aged in dying they would point out that a significant difference between traditional Inuit culture and our own contemporary American culture is that in the Inuit culture there is a belief in a spirit world and a Happy Hunting Grounds to which the aged pass at death, whereas there is no such belief in mainstream American culture. At the same time there is agreement on the underlying value of caring for the aged.

If I may, let me present one more anthropological example where this distinction between beliefs and values is evident and revealing. Among the Dinka people in southern Sudan, in East Africa, certain members of the tribe are regarded as carrying the "life" of the tribe; they are regarded as having various supernatural or divine powers. These are the "masters of the fishing spear," or "spear-masters," as they are called. Through their prayers and incantations they cure the sick, ward off lions, and in general maintain the vitality of the Dinka and their cattle. There are various rituals associated with the spear-masters, but one custom found among the Dinka will seem to us to be repulsive. Over a period of several days, the Dinka dig a hole and after a number of ceremonies, they lower into the hole a spear-master who is still alive. Then the Dinka place cattle dung on the spear-master until the hole is filled and the spear-master is covered except for a narrow opening. The spear-master then slowly suffocates in the cattle dung. This is what we would observe if we were witnesses. Now it should be noted that the spear-masters are buried and expire in this manner when they are quite old, and the ceremony takes place when the spear-masters sense that their end is near. They themselves announce the time of the burial. Moreover, spear-masters understand that when they become spear-masters they will die in this manner. However, informing the Dinka ceremony and practice is a crucial belief. The Dinka believe that unless the spear-master dies in this way the "breath" or life of the people will be lost. If he dies in this ceremonial way his breath passes through the narrow opening and the life of the community, whose culture and economy are centered on cattle-raising, is maintained. The Dinka value the same thing that we do in mainstream American culture: the maintenance of life and the maintenance of the well-being of the community. The difference is over a factual belief about what is necessary to further that end.

Jerry: While the distinction between beliefs and values is important for understanding how societies can have shared values despite their differences, sometimes what masks the fact that societies share values is not a difference in belief, but what may be called a difference in *circumstances*. An example I have read about is provided by Inuit infanticide. In traditional Inuit society infants regularly would be allowed to die of exposure. The killing of infants in our society is of course not only illegal, but is horrendously wrong. It looks as though there is a huge difference in value between Inuit culture and our own culture. But a closer look brings to light a difference in circumstances. In Inuit culture it is common for a mother to nurse her offspring for four years and even longer. Given her share of the work it would be next to impossible for her to nurse more than one child. Remember that the Inuits are nomadic. An Inuit mother when she works outdoors and travels carries her young child under her parka. However, only one child can be cared for this way. Inuit families are like American families in cherishing their children. They would greatly prefer to have the baby they cannot care for adopted by another Inuit couple, and often this happens. But often adoption is not possible and then, in order to care for the children they have, it becomes necessary to kill a newborn, which is usually done simply by exposing the baby to the elements. If this were not done the entire family would be threatened. Such harsh circumstances as these do not exist in our culture, and therefore, we have not needed to face the wrenching choices that traditional Inuit parents had to face. Beneath the different circumstances prevailing in the two cultures there is the shared value of caring for their children and maintaining the family.

Yusuf: So, again, when we dig beneath the superficial cultural differences it turns out that there are moral universals.

Jerry: There are moral universals found in all cultures. And several have been recognized by anthropologists. For instance, they recognize as universals the wrongness of murder and of incest, the prohibition of not telling the truth, the rightness of restitution and reciprocity, and the obligations of parents toward their offspring and of offspring toward their parents.

Vishnu: Well, that's right. Moral universals have been acknowledged, at least by some anthropologists. Even Herskovits allowed that there are cultural universals. He acknowledged that having some form of morality was universal, and so was having a sense of beauty and some standard for truth. Of course Herskovits' acknowledgment that morality is universal in the sense that morality in some form is found in every culture is different from the acknowledgment that there are moral universals in the sense that some specific action, like murder, is universally regarded as wrong or that parents' caring for their children is universally regarded as right and an obligation. It is the latter acknowledgment by anthropologists that Jerry has—correctly—drawn to our attention. However, I remember from my study of anthropology that a distinction was drawn between *moral universals* and *moral absolutes*.

Jerry: What distinction is this, Vishnu?

Vishnu: On the one hand, universal moral values are those values in fact followed or recognized by everyone, or nearly everyone. Everyone in the different societies around the world accepts it as morally right to care for their children, so this is a universal moral value; so too with other values Jerry mentioned. On the other hand, a moral absolute is an unchanging norm or rule that is morally binding on everyone, a moral rule that everyone ought to follow irrespective of social or individual attitudes.

Sarah: What is the difference?

Zainab: I think I see the difference. If everyone thought it was right to be greedy, then being greedy would by definition be a universal value, but it would not for that reason be an absolute value. We would not be under any obligation to become greedy. Or say that all the peoples of the world took it into their heads that female genital mutilation was right; that would not make it a morally binding norm, a moral rule that we ought to follow. It would not make it right to practice female genital mutilation.

Vishnu: We can discover through anthropological observation that parents' caring for their children is universally regarded as right, but discovering that it is an absolute takes something more than these anthropological data. Although as things are it is an anthropological fact that societies universally approve of and require that parents care for their children, if some society for some reason ceased to approve of parents' caring for their children then it would no longer be a universal. But if it were a moral absolute, it would remain a moral absolute—one that that society would be violating.

Sarah: I think I get it. Let's say that it is a universal moral value that parents care for their children. This does not show that cultural moral relativism is false because this universality could be the result of each society approving of parents caring for their children.

Sam: In the same way it does not contradict or disprove subjectivism, for this universality could be the result of each individual feeling that it is right for parents to take care of their children.

Vishnu: Remember how there being different moral beliefs from one society to the next did not prove that cultural moral relativism was correct. Here we see that universal agreement among societies on a moral belief does not disprove cultural moral relativism. And, as Sam says, universal moral agreement among individuals does not disprove subjectivism. By way of contrast, if there were moral absolutes, that would show that both cultural moral relativism and subjectivism are wrong.

Jerry: All right, I see the conceptual difference between universals and absolutes. I was hasty earlier when I said that if either cultural moral relativism or subjectivism were correct, there would be no universal moral values. But is there any reason why a universal could not also be an absolute?

Vishnu: No, they could correspond. Although of course they might not too.

Jerry: It strikes me as morally significant that, say, parent's caring for their children is a universal value and being greedy is not. It is as though an underlying human moral sense was being tapped. I think that the identification of moral universals, *and their being what they are*, points toward their being absolutes, even if it does not prove it.

Vishnu: One thing that has struck me over the years is how much cultures are different and yet the same in many ways.

Yusuf: You know, Vishnu, I have the same sense, which is why I think cultures share universal values. Let me draw upon my personal knowledge in order to say something more about how, despite differences, cultures can share the same underlying moral value. In traditional Islam it is allowable for a man to have up to four wives. Today in some Muslim countries, like Turkey, it is against the law for a man to have more than one wife. In other Muslim countries it is legal, but there are restrictions. In Pakistan, my country, there is a legal requirement that the first wife give her consent in order for a man to take a second wife. Today in Pakistan, there still are polygamous marriages, although there is strong social pressure against a man taking a second wife. So things are changing in Pakistan, while in traditional Islam, and in much of the Muslim world, it remains allowable for a man to have up to four wives. I am modern in my thinking, and probably I would have only one wife.

Zainab: Only "probably"? This is another area of women's rights, and your Aunt Fatima and I need to talk to you about this.

Yusuf: Maybe more than "probably." I haven't seen Aunt Fatima in some time, and, yes, I would like to talk about this with the both of you, and maybe with Uncle Ibrahim too. But please let me continue. I wanted to say something that addresses Vishnu's observation about how much cultures are different and yet the same in many ways. I wish to give an example of this out of my own experience. In the old days the culture in Pakistan was different. My grandfather had three wives and loved each dearly. All of his wives got along; they all felt loved and, while there were some family tensions—as in any family—they respected each other. As a boy I could feel the warmth in my grandfather's home when I went to visit. My grandfather was protective of his family and completely faithful to his wives. For him and for his Muslim culture marital fidelity was a value, but marital fidelity did not mean being true to one woman. Marital fidelity meant a husband's being faithful to his wives—plural—and his wives—plural—being true to him. In America's mainstream culture, of course, marital fidelity is understood as existing between a husband and a wife in a monogamous marriage. So, is my grandfather's Pakistani Muslim culture the same as American culture? Yes, they both value marital fidelity. Are the two cultures different? Yes, since they differ over whether a marital relationship in which a man has more than one wife can embody marital fidelity.

Vishnu: Your example does illustrate the point that had struck me. In light of what you have said about traditional Pakistani Muslim culture we might recall Herskovits' account of polygamous marriage and family life in Dahomey. For Herskovits the family unit in Dahomey is functional, and it is a *family* unit. Though Herskovits reports that tensions and competition among the wives in the family compound can arise, he also says that often a wife will urge her husband to take a second wife. Other writers on social customs in West Africa have commented on how wives in a polygamous family arrangement will urge their husbands to acquire more wives. May we not assume that marital expectations were met and that marital fidelity in its pertinent cultural form was respected in this polygamous family arrangement as well?

Jerry: I think that the same thing may be said about Inuit culture. Yes, there is "wife sharing." Yet within that culture marital expectations are met and there is marital fidelity. It has been observed by Europeans who have lived among the Inuit and come to appreciate their ways that generally married Inuits remain faithful to each other throughout their lives.

Yusuf: The contrast I had in mind was between traditional Pakistani Muslim culture and mainstream American culture, but other cultures may be relevant as well. What strikes me is that when you survey different cultures you will find *universal values* and at the same time differences in the way that these universal values are observed that, *from the standpoint of your own culture*, will seem strange, shocking, and even morally wrong.

5

⚜

Modified Cultural Moral Relativism and Qualified Subjectivism

SETTING: Sam's apartment several days later. Everyone except Shawn is present.

Vishnu: Last time Jerry and Yusuf said that it seemed to them that there are moral universals. And it has seemed that way to some anthropologists too. As we saw last time, the existence of moral universals does not disprove cultural moral relativism or subjectivism. That, however, is not the end of it. Some anthropologists have emphasized that morality is *both* relative and universal. One anthropologist, Robert Redfield, recounted that once when he presented the Inuit practice of assisting in the death of an aged parent as an instance of caring for old parents he was greeted with laughter. Those who laughed were right, he said, for this Inuit practice was different from and opposite to the way they would care for their aged parents. But, he said, he too was right, for the Inuit practice was in fact an expression of care and even tenderness toward aged parents in traditional Inuit culture. In this way, in Redfield's words, "morality is both relative and universal."

Maria: I think I am having some trouble seeing how it could ever be right to help your aged grandfather to hang himself, even if he begged for your help.

Zainab: Yes, and you are not alone, Maria.

45

Jerry: Maybe it will help to bring into our discussion the idea of different levels of description of what people do. Almost always what we do—our actions—can be described in different ways. You could describe what I am doing as "He is sitting in a chair" or as "He is telling us about different levels of description of what people do" or, if you could go into my thoughts, as "He is telling us about different levels of description of what people do, hoping that he will do so with elegant simplicity." All of these descriptions apply. They are all descriptions of the same action. It is just that some descriptions are fuller. A passerby could give the first description. The second requires some understanding of what I am saying, and the last requires some knowledge of my character or at least my hopes.

Maria: Clear enough. How does this help us in understanding the Inuit practice of helping the aged to commit suicide?

Andrew: I think I see how. Recall what Vishnu said last time about how a young Inuit man might assist his grandfather in dying. At one level of description of what the young Inuit man is doing, he is "helping an old man to hang himself." At another level of description his action is properly described as "caring for his aged grandfather."

Jerry: Yes that's right. And notice that it is the *same action* by the young Inuit that is given in both descriptions. The second goes beyond the physical action, or better, beyond the physical level of description. It is more revealing of what the young Inuit man is doing because it incorporates interior aspects of the young Inuit's action, what his intention is.

Zainab: And we would miss this interior level of description altogether if we were limited by an ethnocentric perspective.

Jerry: Right. As we think about the practices of other cultures, then, we can ask several questions. We can ask if those in the other culture share our values, and we can ask if the difference between them and us is a matter of value or, alternatively, a matter of belief or circumstances. Now we see we can ask another question: What is the most revealing description of what they are doing? How does this relate to the Inuit practice? In this way: We can describe the young Inuit man as helping his grandfather to hang himself, and this description invites us in our culture to make the judgment that what he did was wrong. Or we can say that the young Inuit man is caring for his grandfather and what he is doing in helping his grandfather to hang himself *is* caring for his grandfather the best way he knows. It is not only a value he has. It *is* what he is doing.

Andrew: Applying Jerry's point to the Dinka practice of burying alive the spear-master, we can say that what the Dinka people are doing *is* maintaining the life and well-being of the people in the best way they know.

Zainab: And applying it to the Inuit practice of infanticide that was discussed last time, we can say that Inuit parents *are* caring for their children and the family.

Jerry: Yes. Right in both cases.

Maria: So, if I follow what you are saying, Jerry, taking the example of the young Inuit man helping his grandfather to hang himself, under one description what the young Inuit man did was wrong, although under another description it was right. He was wrong to assist his grandfather in committing suicide, but he was right to care for his grandfather. This seems paradoxical.

Jerry: That is not quite what I am saying, Maria, or meant to say. What I mean to say is that the specific action of the young Inuit was right in his culture, but wrong for us in our culture, perhaps because of different beliefs and circumstances, in spite of shared values. At the same time caring for the aged is right in *both* cultures. In fact it is right in all cultures since it is a universal value. Moreover, I would say that it is a moral absolute, but that is another issue.

Vishnu: If Jerry is right, what comes to light here, then, is that there can be shared moral values, even a universal moral value, but nevertheless the *way* the value is acted upon and realized may be right in one culture or society and wrong in another. The specific action of the young Inuit, or the *way* he cares for his grandfather, is wrong in our culture. Even though we can come to understand how the Inuit practice is right in the Inuit culture, and how at one level of description they are doing just as we do—caring for our aged relatives as best we can—it would simply be morally wrong for us, who do not share the Inuits' background beliefs, to assist an aged relative to hang himself.

Sam: But remember, Vishnu, as both you and Jerry noted earlier there is an issue in our American culture about suicide and assisting in suicide. For some in our culture, under certain circumstances, suicide and assisted suicide are permissible, as when the alternative is a life of unbearable pain.

Vishnu: Yes, I recall, Sam. But those who argue that assisting in suicide is permissible to relieve a person from a life of unbearable pain presumably would not argue that assisting in suicide is permissible to relieve a person from boredom and dejection—which was the state of the Inuit grandfather. When I said that it would simply be morally wrong for us in our American culture, who do not share the Inuits' background beliefs, to assist an aged relative to hang himself, I meant an aged relative who was suffering from nothing worse than boredom and dejection. I should have made that clear.

Maria: But what if the Inuits' beliefs about a Happy Hunting Grounds are not true?

Jerry: I don't think that that would matter. In the Inuit case of caring for the aged and in the Dinka case of burying the spear-master, the rightness of what they do is seen only in the light of certain beliefs that they hold, which in turn make the motives and intentions of the Inuit and the Dinka understandable. Now these beliefs, I suspect, are false. I strongly suspect there is no Happy

Hunting Grounds to which the grandfather departs, and I even more strongly suspect that there is no causal connection between the spear-master dying by suffocation in cattle dung and the well-being of the Dinka people. The falsity of what they believe, though, does not destroy the moral rightness of what they are doing at the fuller level of description, a part of which includes motives and intentions. Still, we can believe that with the passage of time and with greater education they will cease to hold these beliefs, and we can even believe that this will be a good thing.

Yusuf: I think that it must be accepted that at the level of more specific description some actions are going to be right in one culture and wrong in another. Let's go back to my example of Islamic marriage. A husband's having more than one wife is right or allowable for Muslims in traditional Pakistani culture, but it is not right for Americans. And here there are no differences in beliefs, as in the Dinka case or the Inuit case of caring for the aged. Nor is there a difference in "circumstances," as in the case of the Inuit practice of infanticide. There was no great hardship in traditional Pakistani culture that required men to take more than one wife. It is more a matter of the marital relationship taking different forms in the traditional Muslim culture of Pakistan and in the American culture.

Sam: I see your point, Yusuf. I can recognize that it is perfectly all right in a traditional Muslim marital relationship, in your grandfather's time at least, and maybe now, for there to be one husband and two or three wives. I can see that that relationship may include mutual respect, love, and faithfulness. At the same time I know that it would be wrong for me to try to enter such a marital relationship with someone I love and marry. It would even be wrong for me to ask her for permission to take a second wife. The marital relationship I would be in has its moral demands, and those demands make it wrong for me to even *think* about having a second woman in my life.

Yusuf: Yes, of course. The Muslim marital relationship with its demands is not one that is really open to you, since you are not Muslim. But in both cultures marital fidelity is a positive moral value.

Sam: So morality is both relative and universal, as Redfield said.

Jerry: But now saying that morality is "relative" does not mean that either subjectivism or cultural moral relativism is correct.

Vishnu: Yes, here saying that morality is "relative" comes to saying that morality is *not the same universally.* So Redfield is saying that morality is and is not universal. This looks like a contradiction, but I don't think it is. In terms of caring for the aged, which is the moral example Redfield used, he is saying that caring for the aged is universal, but caring for them by assisting in their death is not universal. Presumably he would say something similar about marital fidelity and maintaining the family. Each is a universal value, but the manner of respecting that universal value is not universal and so is relative in the sense Redfield is using.

Yusuf: So there are universal moral values and at the same time differences from culture to culture in the way those universal values are realized. The general moral value—like caring for the aged—is universal, but the *expression* of that value is relative to a culture.

Vishnu: I think that is Redfield's point. If it is right, it will apply to a number of universal values: parent's caring for their children, marital fidelity, and, going back to Herodotus, showing a proper respect for our dead fathers.

Sarah: Maybe this is the part of cultural moral relativism that is right. *If we start with a moral universal*, then a society or culture will determine the proper expression of that moral value within that culture.

Jerry: Perhaps this is so. But this is not to say that cultures determine what is morally right and wrong in such a way that, if a culture or society designates some action or practice as right, then that is sufficient to make it right or wrong—which is what cultural moral relativism claims. If we agree with you, Sarah, we are not thereby saying that it is right to persecute a minority in a society if a society says it is right.

Sarah: I agree, and I am not saying that the full thesis of cultural moral relativism is right. In fact, I am inclined to think that it is not right when it is unmodified. At the same time, as we saw, moral universals are compatible with cultural moral relativism and so moral universals in themselves do not show that cultural moral relativism is wrong.

Sam: And the same thing can be said about moral universals and subjectivism.

Vishnu: Yes, I think that you are both right. The existence of moral universals—moral values that are accepted by virtually everyone in the world—is compatible with both cultural moral relativism and subjectivism. In fact, if we define moral relativism as the view that "morality is not universally the same," in the manner that Redfield suggests, then moral relativism in this definition is still compatible with there being moral universals, since the manner of following universal values could be relative to a culture.

Sarah: Yes, that is the view that seems right to me now. There are moral universals, but cultures or societies determine the right way of observing them.

Vishnu: Let's wait a minute. I think I see a problem with even this "modified" cultural moral relativism. If societies can be wrong in what they approve of, they can be wrong about the expression of a moral universal. The society of South Africa approved of apartheid, and those who approved of apartheid may have seen it as an expression of the universal value of maintaining the community. If so, apartheid would turn out to be right according to your modified cultural moral relativism.

Sarah: That cannot be. Maybe it has to be that the way a culture expresses a moral universal must itself be right.

Sam: But then, Sarah, you have surely abandoned cultural moral relativism, for now you are requiring a cultural expression that is right independently of what the culture says—that is, in the light of objective considerations and some transcultural "higher standard."

Sarah: Yes, so it seems.

Jerry: I think that Redfield should have said that morality is both relative and *absolute*. It is absolute in that there are moral absolutes—like caring for the aged—and it is relative in that there can be different expressions of caring for the aged, but those different expressions have to respect the absolute. They cannot be just anything the culture decides.

Sam: But are any moral values absolute?

Jerry: I would say that those universal values identified by anthropologists, and which I named in an earlier discussion we had, are also absolute. They include caring for family, refraining from murder, and telling the truth, you may remember. Here is why I think they are absolute. Regardless of a person's culture, or what that person felt was right, if that person did not care for her or his children, or violated one of the other universals, she or he would be doing something wrong.

Sam: I think I see that caring for the family might be an absolute value, but still I think that there is a place for morally acting on the basis of your moral feeling.

Jerry: So, Sam, you finally give up your subjectivism!

Sam: I am giving up unqualified subjectivism, but I think subjectivism may be right in a qualified form. I think that even if there are moral absolutes, it will be necessary to use our moral feelings to apply them in particular cases.

Maria: Sam may be right. Let me tell you about a case that could illustrate what Sam means. The Mendoza family lives near us, and the Mendozas were faced with a terrible moral decision. Miguel and Rosa, the parents, had two daughters, Elena and Linda. Elena was four and Linda was two. Linda in her second year began to experience liver failure, and the doctors said it would be fatal if left untreated. Miguel and Rosa thought that they could be donors and one of them could give Linda a part of his or her liver, but tests showed that Linda's body would reject liver transplants from her parents. Rejection-suppressing drugs in Linda's case were not workable, the doctors discovered. The doctors then tested uncles and aunts but Linda's body would reject donated livers from anyone in her family. Finally they tested Elena and discovered that she was a possible donor. Linda's body would not reject a portion of her sister's liver. So there was some hope, but the operation would have some danger for Elena. She was only four. Miguel and Rosa had to decide what to do. They thought about what they would tell Elena when she was older and had come to understand that her parents had put her in danger, if they went ahead with the liver transplant. Miguel said he'd have no way to convince her that they had done the right thing. He and Rosa could only hope that Elena would understand that transplanting part of her liver was the only way to save her sister's life and would accept that this was the right thing to do. Miguel and Rosa thought a lot about what to do. There was so much to think about. They prayed a lot too. They finally came to feel that the best thing to do was to go ahead with the transplant operation, and they decided on the basis of their moral feeling to give the doctors permission to perform the operation. A part of Elena's liver was given to Linda. They recognized the absolute value of caring for their children, but when it came to deciding *how* they must do that, they decided on the basis of their feelings.

Sarah: What was the outcome? Did both girls survive?

Maria: Yes, thank heaven.

Sam: I think that in these extreme moral situations qualified subjectivism applies.

Jerry: That was a very tough moral decision, Maria, and it looks as though their decision was an instance of a relativistic choice on the basis of their feelings. It looks like a case where Sam's "qualified subjectivism" applies. But several things give me pause. This would be a case in which there is no clear right decision. Is "qualified subjectivism" going to apply only to such cases? And even in this case there were objective considerations. The operation was necessary to save Linda's life. The operation put Elena in some danger. But the chance that Elena would not survive the liver transplant was less than the chance that Linda would die if the operation were not performed, since it was certain that Linda would die without the transplant. All of these considerations were objective. They did not depend on what anyone felt or thought. Of course this is not to say that they were *decisive*. The Mendozas had to weigh them.

Zainab: And remember, in the case of many moral decisions, there is not the moral uncertainty that there was in Maria's case. Say that Miguel could donate part of his liver to his daughter with no risk, then there would be no moral dilemma and no terrible decision. The one right course is clear, again on the basis of objective considerations.

Also, in Maria's case it is not *arbitrary* moral feelings on the part of the Mendozas that lead to the decision, it is right feelings, by which I mean *rightly formed* moral feelings, informed feelings that the Mendozas struggled to make right in the light of the objective considerations Jerry just mentioned.

Sam: But say that the Mendozas had decided not to risk Elena's life. Would that have been wrong? Would anyone here say that that decision was wrong if they had made it? I don't think so.

Vishnu: Your point is taken, Sam. We should ask what it shows, however. Does it show that whatever moral feelings we come to have decide moral matters in these extreme cases or that in these extreme and horrendous cases morally sensitive persons can come to different judgments after struggling with the objective considerations? In some cases, it may be that either of two courses of action is right and not open to moral condemnation. And in these cases often either decision carries with it something to regret morally. If I were one of the Mendoza parents I would have regretted having to put Elena at risk, and regretted it in a way that would have cost me complete peace of mind. Yet I would have proceeded with hope and trepidation. Indeed there may be times when we do what we have become convinced is the right thing, and we are rightly convinced, yet we still properly regret doing it. The fire captain, whose son is one of those in his command, and who orders his son into a dangerous situation to save fire victims, may well regret giving that order, right as it is. If his son dies or is hurt, he certainly will. But if his son escapes harm, he may still regret having put his son at risk. In this case the right action was clear, for the firefighter's duty is clear. When opposite moral judgments are justified, and neither judgment would be wrong, as in the Mendoza case, the place of regret is all the more evident. But this is not to say that our moral feelings can arbitrarily decide which course of action is right.

Andrew: Think about it this way. Say that there was someone, a comparative stranger, who heard that Linda's life would be saved if a part of Elena's liver was given to Linda. This is all he knows, but he immediately comes to feel that the right thing to do is to perform the transplant operation. He has come to the same decision that the Mendozas came to, but his moral feeling is different from the Mendozas. His feeling, unlike the Mendozas', is formed without reflection and is nearly arbitrary. Using Zainab's idea, we should say that is not a *rightly formed* moral feeling.

Jerry: So again it is *not* moral feelings per se that decide the moral question, but rightly formed moral feelings, if it is moral feelings at all.

Sam: All right. I concede the point. Not all moral feelings are right. I have given up subjectivism. But qualified subjectivism can still be right. When individuals—like the Mendozas—have to decide how to apply a moral absolute, and either of two courses of action would be right, their non-arbitrary, rightly formed moral feelings properly decide the matter. And in these cases there is no *further* "objective" justification of the individual's *preference* of one right course of action over the other. Finally, in these cases at least, sheer preference decides.

Andrew: I can give you an example of what will qualify as sheer preference. I greatly prefer chocolate ice cream to vanilla ice cream and would always choose chocolate over vanilla. Of course this is not a *moral* choice.

Vishnu: Again, as the French say, *"Chacun à son goût,"* each to his or her own taste. In preferring one flavor of ice cream over another *something* like subjectivism applies, but, as Andrew says, here we are not in the realm of morality.

Sam: I see that. Still within morality it seems to me that there are places for unjustified preference. We have seen it in the case of the Mendozas' decision, and we see it in preferring one style of life to another—choosing one "image" of oneself, as Sartre said, or one way of life as a value.

Sarah: Clearly different people choose different styles of life. Some people prefer a quiet life centered on reading and thinking to a more socially active life with many friends. Others make the opposite choice. However, again this is not a moral choice. It is a nonmoral choice of lifestyle.

Andrew: When I first came to this country, I was struck by the fact that Americans drive everywhere. If they have to go two blocks to buy groceries they drive. They could walk, but I guess it is the American lifestyle to drive. Is this another nonmoral choice?

Jerry: If Americans walked more they would be healthier and they would contribute less to world pollution. Maybe there is a *moral* choice here, although it may be debatable whether the choice of lifestyle that involves driving over walking is a moral or nonmoral choice. By contrast, it seems to me that some lifestyles are clearly immoral. A lifestyle that turns around creating, viewing, and propagating child pornography is clearly immoral, for it does not treat others—in this case children—with decent respect. Choosing such a life is to make a moral choice, not a good moral choice but a bad moral choice.

Sam: Yes, I can see that choosing such a lifestyle is to make a morally bad choice. What I was thinking is that there could be several morally good choices open to a person regarding possible lifestyles, and then sheer preference would decide.

Vishnu: Some philosophers have suggested that there is not just one "good life," to which all should aspire, but several, even many, "good lives." They hold that a good life has certain minimum requirements. It must give proper recognition to basic human needs—food and so on—but beyond that there is a range of values that can be drawn upon. For this way of thinking at least some of the values embodied in a good life must be moral values, but different moral values can be at the core of different good lives. A serious person might choose to devote her life to medical research to try to find a cure for malaria or AIDS, or she might choose to become a community activist and social reformer. Each life could be a morally good life.

Sam: Or she could choose to marry and be a good wife, just as a man could choose to marry and be a good husband. This was one of Sartre's "images" or ways of life. Except, contrary to Sartre, if I choose to be a good husband or a research scientist I am not thereby saying it is *the* way of life to be followed by everyone.

Vishnu: Right. And of course, while there may be a number of possible good lives, many will be incompatible. Maybe one could be a good wife or husband *and* a research scientist, but one could not be a full-time research scientist *and* a full-time social reformer. Practically speaking they are incompatible.

Jerry: This is all well and good. However, these good lives that we are referring to are recognizably and objectively good. There is something about each of them that makes it valuable independently of our feelings or our choosing it.

Vishnu: True, but when it comes to choosing among those good or valuable lives *that are morally acceptable,* something like preference decides. And here, and in deciding between two recognizably right courses of action, as in the case of the Mendozas' decision, Sam may be right in his intuition.

Jerry: OK, but we are at this point a long way from cultural moral relativism and subjectivism. It is not what people say—societies or individuals—that makes our actions right or wrong. And we can't make any style of life or "image" morally valuable just by preferring or choosing it. Sam's qualified subjectivism applies only to decisions between courses of action already recognized as objectively morally right, as in the Mendoza case, and to deciding on a valuable life in a range of lives already recognized as objectively good, and Sarah's modified cultural moral relativism applies to the cultural expression that a recognized moral universal will take, and only if the cultural expression is itself objectively right. So if what we mean when we say that "morality is relative" is that moral rightness and wrongness are relative to personal attitudes or to societal or cultural attitudes, it looks like morality just is not relativistic.

6

Moral Relativism versus Moral Absolutism, the Determining Type of Moral Relativism versus the Varying Type, Vishnu Sums Up, and Different Kinds of Cultural Differences Revisited

SETTING: Sam's apartment a week later. Everyone except Shawn is present.

Vishnu: In our discussion of moral relativism we have been focusing on subjectivism and cultural moral relativism. There is another definition of moral relativism that I would like to draw to your attention. Sometimes moral relativism is seen as the denial of "moral absolutism." Understood this way what moral relativism asserts is simply that moral absolutism is false.

Andrew: And what is moral absolutism?

Vishnu: Moral absolutism itself can take several forms. In a primary form, however, moral absolutism is the view that there *are* moral absolutes in the sense of "moral absolutes" that I introduced earlier, namely moral rules or norms that are binding on everyone, which is the sense in which Jerry maintains there are moral absolutes. Moral relativism then becomes the view that there are *no* moral absolutes. So, if there were no moral absolutes, but at most only moral universals, then moral relativism in this form would be right by definition. By contrast, if there were any moral absolutes—if doing no murder or parents' caring for their children were moral absolutes—then moral relativism in this form by definition would be wrong.

Zainab: How does this form of moral relativism relate to subjectivism and cultural moral relativism?

Sarah: I see a difference. This form of moral relativism does not say what morality is relative *to*. It does not say that it is relative to individuals or to cultures.

Vishnu: Right. In fact moral relativism in this form is negatively defined. What it says is simply this: there are no moral absolutes.

Andrew: As we have seen, both subjectivism and cultural moral relativism deny that there are moral absolutes. Both say more than that there are no moral absolutes, but both *imply* that there are no moral absolutes. That is why both would be false if there were moral absolutes, and in this respect both subjectivism and cultural moral relativism are like moral relativism defined as the view that there aren't any moral absolutes.

Vishnu: There are two other forms of moral absolutism worth noting. Each, like this first form, is opposed to a form of moral relativism that is negatively defined in terms of the form of moral absolutism that it denies, and each is at odds with both subjectivism and cultural moral relativism. But many who reject forms of moral relativism on the grounds that there are moral absolutes would also reject these two forms of moral absolutism. To put it another way, one could reject different forms of moral relativism—including cultural moral relativism and subjectivism—without accepting either of these two forms of moral absolutism.

The first of these two other forms of moral absolutism is the position that there is one "absolute" standard that defines true morality, one overarching moral standard that determines moral rightness for all persons whenever and wherever they live or have lived. It is opposed to and denies moral relativism which is understood as the view that there is *no* absolute moral standard, and of course it denies both subjectivism and cultural moral relativism.

Sam: In the class that Sarah, Jerry, and I took I remember that we read a philosopher, John Stuart Mill, who said that there was one fundamental "standard" for moral rightness.

Sarah: That's right. I remember it because it sounded pretty good to me, at least initially. Mill's standard, or "criterion" as he sometimes called it, is that right actions produce happiness, and so the best action that we can perform in any situation is the one that will produce the *most* happiness for all concerned.

Jerry: In the same class, as I remember, another very different absolute standard for moral rightness was put forward by the German philosopher Immanuel Kant. Let me see if I can remember it. It is something like this: unless you can coherently "will" that what you are about to do is all right for everyone to do, it is wrong. And he thought that lying would be wrong because if it was all right for everyone to lie that would make anyone's lying pointless, since lying would be expected by others. So one could not coherently "will" lying to be universally allowable.

Vishnu: Not bad, Jerry! Kant's standard is hard to get just right. Both Mill's and Kant's standards are open to question. They both have been criticized as well as defended. But we do not need to get into the question of their validity in order to observe that *if* either were correct, then there would be an absolute moral standard, which would mean that subjectivism and cultural moral relativism are wrong.

Yusuf: Are these two the only possible absolute moral standards?

Vishnu: No, other absolute standards have been proposed. Many have seen their religion as embodying an absolute moral standard. However, there is a third form of moral absolutism, which stands opposed to moral relativism. This third form of moral absolutism is the position that there are absolute norms in the sense of *exceptionless norms*.

Sam: What does "exceptionless norm" in this context mean?

Vishnu: Let's start with "norm" and remind ourselves of what it means. This is the term I used earlier as another expression for "moral rule." As a moral rule a norm simply states what we "ought" to do or not do; norms state our moral obligations or, as some say, our moral duty. The moral rule or norm "it is wrong to lie" indicates a moral obligation not to lie.

Maria: I would think that everyone of mature age, except perhaps some sociopaths, accepts that we have obligations to one another.

Vishnu: Yes, I think so. And we should observe that relativists do not dispute that there are moral obligations. It's just that, for relativists, obligations are relative to the individual or to a culture, or in some other way relative.

Sam: Norms are just moral rules, then. But what does "exceptionless" mean?

Vishnu: That is a little harder to explain, but, finally, it's not that difficult to understand. Most of us appreciate that our obligations can conflict. Say that Kavita—my wife—asked me to retrieve some papers from her office that she needs, and I said I would. I have to rush because her office is about to close. On my way to her office, I come upon a man on the sidewalk who is unconscious. I have an obligation to my wife, but also I have an obligation to help the man who is unconscious. My obligations conflict in that I cannot keep both of them. If I help the man I will not be able to get my wife's papers, and if I go ahead to the office I will not help the man unconscious on the sidewalk.

Jerry: It is obvious that you should help the unconscious man. He could be in danger of dying. If this situation actually occurred, I'm sure that Kavita would understand when you explained.

Vishnu: I suppose that almost everyone would agree with your judgment, Jerry. In cases where obligations conflict, we try to keep the obligation that is more important, the superior obligation. Many times, as in my simple example, it is clear which obligation is superior and overrides the other, although sometimes it is not at all clear which obligation is superior—as in Maria's case of the Mendozas' decision. Still, in many cases it is clear which obligation is superior. And the superior obligation overrides the lesser obligation. This is the way many of us think.

Yusuf: I think I see where you are going, Vishnu. In the conflict-of-obligations case you have presented there is an exception to your obligation to do what you told your wife you would do. So there is an exception to the norm "it is right to do what you say you will do."

Jerry: Remember the case we discussed from Inuit culture. The moral norm here should be expressed as "it is right to do what you *commit yourself* to doing." In our culture when we say we will do something, generally we commit ourselves to doing it. As we saw, in Inuit culture these words—or the Inuit words that some would translate this way—do not amount to making such a commitment.

Yusuf: I accept your emendation, Jerry. With it in place, Vishnu's conflict-of-obligations case contains an exception to the norm "it is right to do what you commit yourself to doing."

Vishnu: Yes, you have the idea, Yusuf. In our moral thinking most of us allow that many if not all of the moral norms or rules we follow admit of exceptions in conflict situations, and so we allow the norms we follow are *not* exceptionless. The third form of absolutism holds that our moral norms, or moral rules, *are* exceptionless.

Sarah: If our obligations admit of exceptions, doesn't that mean that they are not moral absolutes?

Vishnu: We have to be careful here. A moral absolute is a value—an obligation—that is binding on everyone. It extends to everyone, so no one can correctly say "I do not have that obligation." Thus if caring for one's children is a moral absolute, then everyone has an obligation to care for their children, regardless of culture or idiosyncratic feelings. However, this is not to say that a moral absolute is exceptionless. To claim that it is exceptionless is to make a further claim.

Yusuf: Well of course! If we think about it, we can see that even if there are moral absolutes, they could conflict. Our obligation to care for our children and our obligation to care for the elderly may be absolutes. Most often, thank goodness, we can keep both obligations. Yet, they clearly could conflict— even if each is an absolute. Or take the obligation not to lie and the obligation to protect life. They may both be absolutes, but they can conflict. Say that a madman or a man in a rage was seeking to kill someone under our protection. Our shielding the person under our protection and throwing the madman off the scent might well require us to lie. It is clear that not lying can be an absolute moral value that is binding on everyone and at the same time *not* be an absolute norm because it admits of exceptions and so is not exceptionless.

Vishnu: Your case is interesting, Yusuf, because Kant who thought that there was an absolute moral standard also thought that moral norms are exceptionless, and one norm that he names is the one against lying.

Sam: Let me see if I get all this about moral absolutism. It can take three forms. They are related but different. First, there is the view that there are moral absolutes. Second, there is the view that there is one absolute moral standard. And third, there is the view that moral norms or rules are absolute in the sense of being exceptionless. If any one of these three forms of moral absolutism were somehow proven true, that would disprove the specific form of moral relativism that is its opposite. But, moreover, each form of moral absolutism would disprove both subjectivism and cultural moral relativism.

Jerry: So one could reject subjectivism and cultural moral relativism on the basis of there being moral absolutes or on the basis of there being an absolute standard or on the basis of there being exceptionless moral norms, which would be absolute norms in this sense. But to do so on the basis of the first does not commit one to the other two. And some who accept that there are moral absolutes *reject* the idea that there is an absolute moral standard and the idea that there are exceptionless moral norms.

Vishnu: That last point is right, Jerry. And you and Sam are right that *if* moral absolutism in any of these three forms could be proven, then that would disprove both subjectivism and cultural moral relativism. But proving absolutism in any of these three forms is not easy. Take the first form: that there are moral absolutes. Here we have to remember proving that caring for your child is an absolute requires more than proving it is a universal value. And this is not easy. Consider the second form: that there is one absolute standard. The search for a single absolute moral standard is, if anything, more difficult than proving there are moral absolutes. Not everyone accepts the absolute standards proposed by Mill or Kant. In fact they are incompatible, so no one could consistently accept both. At one time it was accepted by many that the will of God provides an absolute standard, but in our age of religious skepticism it is no longer viable to cite God as the source of an absolute standard. So it has been claimed. Lastly, take the third form of moral absolutism: that moral norms or rules are exceptionless. Many reject this form because it seems obvious that in conflict-of-obligations cases one obligation will override the other—as in my example of my obligation to Kavita to retrieve papers from her office—and this means that at least some norms are not exceptionless.

Andrew: I can see that proving moral absolutism in any of its three forms could be difficult, and it seems to me that the third form is especially doubtful. However, the second form—that there is an absolute standard—seems to hold more promise. Say that one has faith in God and accepts God's commands as the absolute standard for moral rightness. Wouldn't that person have a reason for thinking there *is* an absolute standard and so a reason for rejecting moral relativism?

Maria: I think that she or he would.

Vishnu: Yes, such religious believers would have a reason to reject moral relativism as the denial of an absolute standard and to reject moral relativism in the forms we have discussed, subjectivism and cultural moral relativism. In fact, such religious believers would have to reject them in order to be consistent. Their reason for rejecting moral relativism, however, might not carry much weight for those who do not share their faith.

Jerry: In my religious tradition, which is a fairly strict form of Christianity, we look to the Bible for moral direction, and we understand that the word of God is an absolute moral standard. As you know I am *very* suspicious of moral relativism, to put it mildly, and I do believe that there are moral absolutes as well as an absolute moral standard consisting of God's word. However I have not argued that moral relativism—subjectivism and cultural moral relativism—are wrong *because* they deny either moral absolutes or an absolute moral standard. That would beg the question. Instead I have, along with Zainab, argued against moral relativism on independent grounds. Let's not forget those arguments that Zainab and I presented against cultural moral relativism, arguments that also apply to subjectivism. If those arguments were good before they are still good; and they provide their own reasons for rejecting cultural moral relativism and subjectivism.

Vishnu: Jerry is right. If those arguments that he and Zainab presented were good—logically good—before, they still are good. Remember, though, while they presuppose, and imply, some "higher standard" by which cultural moral beliefs, and individual moral feelings, can be judged, such a higher standard might be human rights or respect for persons or some other higher standard. It need not be a single absolute standard.

Jerry: I did not mean to deny that point, Vishnu. Those arguments disprove moral relativism, but they do not prove the moral absolutism that I think is correct. I concede that.

Sarah: In my religious tradition, too, it is accepted that God's law is the absolute standard for right action. The basis and authority for morality reside in God, and we believe that God's law in the form of his commandments is in the Torah as it was given to Moses.

Sam: I am less observant in my Judaism than Sarah. I think that the Bible provides some moral instruction, but I do not believe that it contains an absolute moral standard.

Jerry: Sarah, if you accept God's law as the absolute standard for moral rightness, then why were you defending cultural moral relativism?

Sarah: Well, I thought that it was the better of the two forms of moral relativism we were discussing. I thought the cultural form was better than the individual form, and, anyway, I have conceded that cultural moral relativism is wrong in its unmodified form.

Zainab: Yes, but will even your modified form work if God's law is the absolute standard?

Sarah: I think so. I am not sure.

Vishnu: Remember the problem we saw before with your modified cultural moral relativism regarding apartheid. It is even more acute if you regard maintaining the community as a part of God's law. Unless you think of apartheid as being in accord with God's law, which I doubt.

Sarah: No, of course I don't. It must be that the cultural expression of following God's law is itself in accord with God's law. But now, I see, I have departed from cultural moral relativism. Still, if the culture does not violate God's law in determining its expression of following God's law, its cultural expression can be right. Maybe, finally, this is what seemed to me to be right about cultural moral relativism, even if, strictly, this is not what it is saying.

Zainab: Like Sarah, I too accept God's law as the absolute moral standard. However, it is evident that there is room to disagree about what the *shari'a* or divine law demands. For some it demands the repression of women. Such a view of God's law is really against Islam, I believe.

Sarah: In Judaism too there can be discussions of what God's law requires.

Jerry: The same holds in Christianity. It is apparent that people can agree that God's law is an absolute standard, but disagree about what God's law morally requires. For instance, some Christians feel that all war is against God's law and wrong and some feel that some wars are justified.

Vishnu: Of course while some differences of belief about what God's law requires can be found *within* a religious tradition—within Christianity, Judaism, or Islam—other differences of belief about what God's law requires can be found *between* religious traditions. Yusuf's example of polygamous marriage being allowed within Islam, as opposed to Judaism and Christianity, is an example. Let me say, though, echoing what I said time before last, that in my travels in societies that are predominantly Jewish, Christian, or Islamic—or Hindu or Buddhist, or other religions, for that matter—I have been struck by how much that is valued is the same beneath the superficial differences.

Sarah: Yes, I can believe that, Vishnu. There are moral universals, after all. Going back to Zainab and Jerry's arguments, there is something else to be noted. The existence of such a higher standard—the sort presupposed by those arguments—would mean that moral rightness is objective in the sense that it is not determined by personal or cultural attitudes, Jerry's sense of "objective." But also if God's commands or law gave us an absolute standard, moral rightness would be objective.

Andrew: And moral rightness would be objective if either Mill's or Kant's absolute standard were correct.

Jerry: So, if there is an absolute standard—like God's law—then morality is objective and the form of relativism that denies an absolute standard is wrong, and so are subjectivism and cultural moral relativism. But if we set aside the issue of whether there is an absolute standard, still subjectivism and cultural moral relativism are wrong. They are wrong because there are "higher standards" of the sort presupposed by the arguments Zainab and I offered, which themselves make morality objective. I think that we can finally set aside subjectivism and cultural moral relativism.

Vishnu: I doubt that every subjectivist and cultural moral relativist would agree with you, Jerry, but your judgment seems to reflect the consensus of our group. However, before we get too comfortable I want to suggest that there is another very different way to think about moral relativism. Tonight we have considered moral relativism in a negative definition. Defined negatively, moral relativism is the view that "moral absolutism" is false. Since moral absolutism can be understood in any of the three different ways we have discussed, moral relativism defined as the denial of moral absolutism would amount to one of three negative views: the view that there are no moral absolutes, the view that there is no one absolute moral standard, or the view that there are no exceptionless moral norms or rules.

Earlier, though, in all our previous evenings of discussion, we considered moral relativism in two forms that take a positive definition: subjectivism and cultural moral relativism. Subjectivism and cultural moral relativism provide an answer to the question "What *determines* moral rightness and moral wrongness?" For this reason they both belong to what may be called the "determining type" of moral relativism. Subjectivism names the feelings or beliefs or choices of the individual—an individual "attitude"—as what determines moral rightness and wrongness for that individual. This, of course, makes morality relative to the individual. Cultural moral relativism names customs or societal beliefs about what is morally right or wrong—a cultural "attitude"—as what determines moral rightness and wrongness for the members of a culture or society. And this makes morality relative to a culture or society. In our conversations about moral relativism, we have primarily considered these two forms of determining moral relativism—subjectivism and cultural moral relativism—and this is not accidental. They are the forms that naturally come forward for consideration.

Sarah: Are these the only forms of the determining type of moral relativism?

Vishnu: There could be others. One might cite, not the individual or culture, as the determiner of moral rightness but the family or clan. Such forms of moral relativism would be like cultural moral relativism in that they would regard some *group attitude* as what determines moral rightness and wrongness, just as cultural moral relativism does. It is just that the group appealed to would be smaller than a culture or society. In theory there could be other forms as well. One philosopher has suggested that what it is right or wrong for us to do is relative to an "agreement" we have with others. Different people might have different agreements with others. If we were members of a mafia "family" our agreement might make it wrong to kill members of the "family" but allow the killing of outsiders. In the case of this form of moral relativism, it is the agreement that determines the rightness or wrongness of what we do.

Jerry: I have a feeling that you have another shoe to drop Vishnu. You mentioned another "type" of moral relativism. What is it?

Vishnu: By way of contrast to the determining type of moral relativism there is a completely different type of moral relativism: the "varying type." The varying type of moral relativism says that moral rightness and wrongness can vary. There is no single true morality, or put positively, there is more than one true morality, which means that what is right, in the sense of being morally required, for one person may not be morally required for another, and what is morally allowable for one person may be wrong for another.

Andrew: This sounds like the definition of moral relativism as "morality is not universally the same," which we got from Redfield.

Vishnu: Except that the view suggested by Redfield allows that the proper expression of a moral universal would be determined by a culture.

Andrew: For this "varying type of moral relativism," as you call it, what makes right actions right and wrong actions wrong?

Vishnu: Well, it is not what a culture says, as it is for cultural moral relativism. The varying type of moral relativism can accept those arguments against cultural moral relativism that Jerry and Zainab gave us. In the same way it can accept it that similar arguments can be directed against subjectivism. Beyond this, the varying type of moral relativism, in itself, has no positive thesis about what determines what is right for you or me or other people. In this it is unlike subjectivism and cultural moral relativism, which do have such a thesis. The varying type simply affirms that there is no single true morality, which means that some action can be right for you and wrong for me. So, for the varying type, while we have obligations, sometimes what is an obligation for me may not be an obligation for the next person. And, while the varying type allows that there are objective reasons why some action is wrong for me, those reasons may not make that action wrong for the next person.

Here is a simple example. Kavita is flying to India tomorrow, and she is depending on me to take her to the airport. I am her husband, and if I failed her in this she would rightfully be morally disappointed in me. It would be wrong for me to go to the cinema just when she is expecting me to drive her to the airport. However, it would not be wrong for Andrew or Sam to go to the cinema tomorrow instead of driving my wife to the airport.

Jerry: I think I get it. There are lots of examples of that kind. Any time I promise someone to do something, if I fail to do the thing I promised I would do what is wrong. However the next person, who made no such promise, would not do what is wrong if he or she did not do the thing that *I* promised I would do.

Maria: I am not married and have no children. But if I were a parent I'd have an obligation to provide care for my children. If I were a lax parent and did not provide care for my children, I would not be doing what is right. Others would not have this obligation to care for *my* children, and they would not be doing what is wrong if they did not provide parental care for my children. I believe that we all have some kind of obligation to care for the children of the world, but that is different. I am speaking here of *parental* care.

Vishnu: These are pertinent examples and illustrate how what is right or morally permissible for one person can be wrong for another.

Sarah: These are examples of different personal obligations and differences in what is permissible for individuals. Are there cultural examples as well?

Yusuf: The example I provided earlier is a cultural example. In the Muslim culture of Pakistan, and in other Muslim cultures, it is morally allowable to have more than one wife, but not so in American culture. And there are similar examples when we contrast traditional Inuit culture and American culture.

Sarah: This sounds like cultural moral relativism, but I can see that it is not. It is one thing to say that what is right in one culture is wrong in another culture, and it is a different thing to say that what is right in one culture and wrong in another is *determined* by what those cultures say. This is a point that has become clear to me, and so we might reject—even disprove—cultural moral relativism and still recognize that some things that are right in one culture are wrong in another.

Jerry: In the same way it is clear that if *both* of the forms of the determining type of moral relativism that we have considered are wrong, still the varying type could be right.

Zainab: So the varying type says that what is right or morally allowable for one person may be wrong for another person. Does this varying type of moral relativism allow that some things are accepted as right by everyone? Does it deny that there are moral universals? And does it deny moral absolutes?

Vishnu: The varying type of moral relativism does not deny that many things are accepted as right by everyone. Being honest, parents' caring for their children, and other moral values, could be moral universals. It can accept all those moral universals that we talked about earlier. They could even be absolutes, be real and binding moral obligations for all, so that, in the absence of an overriding obligation, if anyone failed to be honest or to care for her or his children that person would be doing what is morally wrong.

Yusuf: If this form of relativism allows moral absolutes, does it allow that there can be different ways of meeting our absolute obligations? Do all loving parents have to care for their children in exactly the same way?

Vishnu: This view allows that across cultures and even within a culture there can be different ways parents can and ought to care for their children. One child may be nurtured when she is made to practice the violin for hours a day, while another child is not. For this view, the form of parental caring that is right to follow can vary from one family to another.

Jerry: So the varying type of moral relativism is different from the determining type in that it has no thesis about what determines moral rightness. But, as you said, Vishnu, it does recognize or allow different moral *reasons* why an action is right for someone. For instance, a person has made a promise to do something or a person is the parent of children, or parents see that intense violin practice will nurture their child. And there could be other reasons, of course: a person is in a position to help someone in urgent need. These reasons might apply to one person and not to another, and so what is right for one person, what is morally required of one person, may not be morally required of another.

Andrew: Yes, for the varying type of moral relativism moral rightness can "vary" in that what is right in the sense of morally required of one person may not be morally required of the next person. Also the reasons why an action is right can "vary." If we ask of this varying type of moral relativism "What is morality relative *to*?" its reply will be "It varies."

Vishnu: You may be right, Andrew. Is this a weakness of the view?

Andrew: I am not sure. If the varying type of moral relativism allows different reasons why actions can be right, doesn't that take away morality's objectivity?

Sarah: I don't think it does. It still allows that morality is objective, for it recognizes moral reasons that are objective in that they do not depend on what people—individuals or societies—say or believe. It is an objective fact if a promise was made or if I am a parent. It is even an objective fact what the expectations of the marital relationships in a society are.

Jerry: It is not an internal part of varying moral relativism that there are moral absolutes—values and obligations that apply to and morally bind everyone—but, as Vishnu says, this form of moral relativism "can accept" moral absolutes. Can it also accept an absolute standard for moral rightness?

Maria: Can it accept God's law as the absolute standard?

Vishnu: You and Jerry raise a difficult question, Maria. Perhaps it will depend on the proposed absolute standard, but let us take God's law as the absolute standard.

Sarah: I think that the varying type of moral relativism and God's law being an absolute standard can go together because people can disagree about what God's law requires of us. In my religious tradition there can be disagreements about what God's law requires. Zainab said that the same occurs in Islam, and Jerry said such disagreements could be found in Christianity. And, of course, there can be disagreements across religious traditions.

Vishnu: Unfortunately this fact of disagreement about what God's law requires does not answer the question that Maria and Jerry have raised.

Sarah: Why not?

Vishnu: Because the question is: Can there be an absolute standard—or for our focused form of the question, can God's law be an absolute standard—and still what is morally required of one person not be morally required of another, so that the varying type of moral relativism would be right? Put another way, the question is whether God's law can be an absolute standard and people following it have different obligations. The question is not whether people can disagree about what God's law requires, but about what obligations it creates.

Zainab: So the question is not whether within Islam Muslims can disagree about what God's law requires, or whether Muslims and those in another religious traditions, like Christianity, can disagree about what God's law requires. The question is whether Muslims can have different obligations from one another, or Muslims and Christians have different obligations, *if* God's law is the absolute standard.

Vishnu: Yes, Zainab, I think your formulation captures the issue rather well.

Maria: Maybe this example from my Catholic tradition will help. My tradition allows that there are different ways to serve God and to follow God's law. If a man becomes a priest and takes a vow of celibacy, then he has an obligation not to have sexual relations. But this obligation of course does not hold for lay people who may follow God's law in marrying and raising a family.

Sarah: In my religious tradition, certainly in my form of Judaism, it is a requirement that the dietary laws be strictly followed, but this is not a requirement for Christians, who follow God's law in their own way.

Jerry: There is another, complimentary, way of thinking about this question. We have recognized that if I make a promise I have an obligation to do what I promised, but the next person, who did not make this promise, does not have this obligation. This seems as clear as day. Surely this fact does not contradict the idea that God's law is the absolute moral standard. It must follow, then, that God's law being the absolute standard does allow that what is an obligation for one person may not be an obligation for another, and so it allows that the varying type of moral relativism can be right.

Vishnu: The varying form of moral relativism also allows that in some cases where a moral decision has to be made, especially in cases of a truly terrible moral dilemma, there may be no *single* right decision. We saw this in the case of the Mendozas' moral dilemma. They made a morally defensible decision, but if they had decided not to expose Elena's life to risk, that decision, as Sam helped us see, would not be wrong.

Yusuf: Is this possibility of two incompatible decisions both being right in accord with an absolute standard?

Maria: I think so. A young Catholic man may have to decide between taking the path that leads to becoming a priest and not doing so but marrying and having a family instead. Either path may be a right path. Each is in accord with God's law.

Jerry: Last time we considered how there might be a number of possible "good lives." Two we mentioned were being a research scientist seeking a cure for AIDS or some other disease and being a social reformer. One could pursue one or the other but not both. Either could be a way of seeking the good or of loving one's neighbor in accord with God's law. So here too God's law being the absolute standard allows that each of two incompatible decisions is right.

Maria: There may be lots of examples. Imagine a young woman who is asked by each of two young men to marry him. She can't decide. She should marry the one she loves, but she is attracted to both. Finally she decides. It is not morally wrong for her to marry the one she decides upon, but it also would not have been morally wrong for her to marry the other man who proposed. Neither choice violates God's law.

Jerry: Well, this type of moral relativism may be acceptable, but I think that it is very weak. It allows that there are moral absolutes and even an absolute standard.

Vishnu: Granted. At the same time, though, it captures what seems to many to be right about moral relativism. It acknowledges that what is right and morally required for some people may not be morally required of others and that what is wrong for one person may not be wrong for another person—across cultures and within cultures. It acknowledges that people in difficult moral situations—like that facing the Mendozas—can decide to do different things and yet both are doing what is right.

Sam: I have been thinking about what started our discussion that first night a couple of weeks ago and the different types of moral relativism that we have been talking about tonight. That first night we were talking about a hard moral decision that Jean-Louis faced in the movie *The Decision*. It was the same decision that one of Jean-Paul Sartre's students had to make, in the case Sartre gives us in his *Existentialism is a Humanism*. Sartre and his student were in Nazi-occupied France. And Sartre's student had to decide between staying in France and taking care of his mother, and going to England and joining the Free French Forces to fight the occupiers.

I would like to go back to the moral decision that Sartre's student had to make and re-examine it in light of the different types of moral relativism we now have before us.

Maria: A question we did not ask that first night is: What will happen to his mother if he leaves her?

Sam: Sartre says that she lived only for her son and that his departure "would plunge her into despair."

Maria: I think that it matters a lot how much his mother will miss him, and on whether she has the support of others in her family.

Yusuf: What if Sartre's student does join the Free French Forces in England. Will he be able to make a real contribution?

Sam: It is not clear. Sartre observes that there is a chance that he will be detained in Spain on his way to England or that he will be stuck in an office if he gets to England.

Jerry: One thing to notice is that Sartre did not give us a wide open case in which anything his student chooses is as right as any other thing. The student's choice is between two courses of action: stay and take care of his mother or join the Free French Forces in England, and, we might observe, he has a recognizable obligation to do both. It seems to me that we can imagine objective reasons making one choice or the other clearly right. Say that the student's mother has wide family support, and there is a good chance that the student will reach England and he has badly needed skills that will enhance the efforts of the Free French Forces, communications skills, for instance. Then it is pretty clear that he ought to join the Free French Forces. Or alternatively, say that his mother is in grave danger of falling into deep despair if her son leaves and she depends on him alone, and say that the chances are excellent he won't get to England and even if he does he has nothing special to contribute. Then it is clear that he ought to stay in France with his mother.

Vishnu: Is no one going to mention the moral consideration that all war is wrong?

Sam: Some people believe that all war is wrong, but Sartre didn't and I don't. I don't suppose that Sartre's student was Jewish. But say he was. Then he would have a strong moral reason to fight against the Nazis, for they were killing millions of Jews in their camps in what was the Holocaust. In fact this would be a strong moral reason for Sartre's student to fight the Nazis whether or not he is Jewish. Yet, even so, there might be a strong moral reason for his staying with his mother and protecting her, especially if she was Jewish.

Vishnu: I understand what you are saying, Sam. Let us set aside the question of the morality of war.

Jerry: So let's see where we are. Setting aside the question of the morality of war, we can identify a number of objective factors that are morally relevant: whether the student's mother depends on him alone for support and protection, whether there is family support that would be sufficient for her protection and care in his absence, the likelihood of the student's reaching England, and the value of the contribution he would make to the efforts of the Free French Forces if he did get to England. Allowing that he has an obligation to care for his mother *and* an obligation to fight against the Nazi occupiers, it appears that, depending on the configuration of these factors, either obligation might turn out to be superior.

Andrew: But there is another possibility. It is possible that neither course of action is clearly *the* right thing to do. There are objective considerations, but they might not clearly decide the matter.

Maria: In that case, it would be more like the decision the Mendozas had to face.

Jerry: If the scenario of the decision that Sartre's student has to make should turn out in this way to be parallel to the decision the Mendozas made, then either decision could be right and neither should be seen as wrong.

Vishnu: Yes, although there may be something for the student to regret, whichever decision he makes. For one way he will be leaving his mother, and the other way he will not be supporting the Free French Forces. But it remains that if we were right in what we said about the Mendozas' decision, and Sartre's student's decision is parallel, then neither decision by Sartre's student would be wrong.

Sam: This is like what I thought at first when I said that morality is relative, but also it is different. I thought that if Jean-Louis in *The Decision* or Sartre's student made a sincere choice or really felt that his choice was right, he would be doing what is right whichever choice he made. But I have come to see that Sartre's student's doing what is right is not just a matter of choosing or feeling it is right. There are right feelings and wrong feelings, as Zainab said. Yet I was right in a sense, at least in the sense that in Sartre's case it *could be* that whether the student decides to stay with his mother or to join the Free French Forces, he would do what is right.

Vishnu: You may be right, Sam. If you are, it is because, in one way, morality is relative. Under certain circumstances, moral rightness can vary.

Jerry: But this is not to say that subjectivism is right after all.

Sam: I see that, Jerry. I now think, to use Vishnu's terms, that the moral rightness of the decision that Sartre's student had to make is relative in the "varying" sense, not in the "determining" sense.

Jerry: It seems to me that it is important that Sartre's student is facing a moral dilemma. If all the morally relevant factors—all the objective considerations—were on one side, we would not have this "varying" of moral rightness.

Vishnu: I sometimes wonder if all our moral decisions are made in the face of a moral dilemma so that whatever we decide someone is morally hurt. However, even if this is so, not every moral decision amounts to the serious kind of moral dilemma that Sartre's student faced.

Sam: You know, the moral dilemma faced by Sartre's student is not the only serious one we have had before us.

Vishnu: Yes, there is the hard dilemma faced by the Mendozas.

Sam: And there is another. One closer to home. I am thinking of the one that Shawn made me face when the police came to my door looking for him. At the time things happened so quickly I just reacted. Later I thought about what I had done and how I felt about it.

Andrew: There could be a number of things to think about, a number of morally relevant considerations. For instance, why were the police looking for Shawn?

Sam: They were looking for him because he sells drugs. I have known Shawn since high school. These days we don't see each other much, but we are friends. Even in high school he did a little dealing. These days he has his spot on a particular corner, and a number of wealthy clients from uptown come down to buy cocaine from him. Usually the police do not bother him, but occasionally there is a crack down, and that's what happened that night.

Jerry: What do you think about his being a cocaine supplier?

Sam: I have urged him to quit. He is really a bright guy, but he has never developed his abilities. I can't count the times I have tried to convince him that he owes it to himself to make something of himself. It is just a question of time before the police arrest him.

Jerry: And then there is the danger in which he puts his friends who help him. Also he is contributing to all those evils that go with drug trafficking. Maybe his wealthy clients are not suffering, but there are plenty of victims.

Vishnu: As long as we are thinking about what is morally relevant, there is another consideration. Socrates argued that those who live in a state and benefit from the protection of the state's laws owe it to the state to obey its laws.

Sam: I can see the moral relevance of all these factors. And I agree that they are "objective," as Jerry would say. But, I don't see myself turning my friend over to the police.

Jerry: Still, maybe you ought to.

Zainab: As Sam said, he has a dilemma.

Maria: Yes, Sam has a dilemma, and that means that there are moral considerations on the other side. There is such a thing as loyalty to your friends.

Jerry: I agree. But just what does that loyalty require? Maybe turning in Shawn is the best thing you can do for him.

Sam: I wonder about that. All I can say is that I am glad that the night the police came to my door is behind me and I have time to sort all this out. So where are we on moral relativism? We have covered a lot of ground, and there have been several turns that the issues have taken. Vishnu, could you give us a summary of all we have discussed these last several weeks about moral relativism?

Vishnu: I believe that I can sum up. Let me try. Early on, the first night of our discussion, we distinguished between subjectivism and cultural moral relativism. Each makes morality relative to what people say or believe or feel.

Subjectivism makes morality relative to an individual or personal attitude, and cultural moral relativism makes morality relative to a societal or cultural attitude.

We considered an argument for cultural moral relativism that argues from differences in cultural moral beliefs to cultural moral relativism, but that argument, we found, did not establish cultural moral relativism.

Then Zainab and Jerry presented us with three related but different arguments against cultural moral relativism, one hinged on meaningfully comparing cultural moral beliefs as to which is better; another had to do with individuals in a society being able to question the moral beliefs of their society or culture in a meaningful way; and the third had to do with the possibility of a change in a society's moral beliefs for the better. If any of these arguments is logically good, it shows that cultural moral relativism is false.

All of these arguments presuppose *some* "higher standard" by which cultural or societal moral beliefs could be judged. Among the candidates for such a higher standard are human rights, the general welfare of society, the fair and equal treatment of all the members of the society, and having a decent respect for each member of the society. All of these standards are "objective" in the sense that Jerry gave us. Although the arguments presented by Zainab and Jerry presuppose some higher standard, I tried to show how the higher standard presupposed by these arguments need not be the one and only standard by which a culture's moral beliefs might be judged. And these same arguments, we saw, could be adapted to apply to subjectivism. So if they show cultural moral relativism to be false, they also show subjectivism to be false.

We went on to distinguish between moral universals, which some anthropologists recognize, and moral absolutes, which are norms that are morally binding on everyone. Subjectivism and cultural moral relativism are logically compatible with the first, but not with the second.

We came to see that, with the avoidance of ethnocentrism, we might recognize a number of shared moral values that could be universals. Also we came to see that there could be a moral universal, or even a moral absolute, observed by different societies and nevertheless the expression of that moral universal, or absolute, might be different in the two cultures; it could even be that the expression in one culture would be wrong in the other culture. Herodotus' Greeks and Callatians both honored the dead, but the way the one did it would be atrocious and wrong in the other culture. This does not reinstate cultural moral relativism because, as Sarah observed earlier this evening, it is one thing to say that what is right in one culture is wrong in another culture, and it is a different thing to say that what is right in one culture and wrong in another is *determined* by what those cultures say so that *whatever* a society calls right *is* right.

Similarly, we saw that when it came to choosing between "good lives" it could finally come down to individual preference, and in at least some cases of moral dilemmas, either of two moral choices could be right. However, again, this does not reinstate subjectivism.

We went on to explore the opposition between moral relativism and moral absolutism. This time-honored, but not exclusive, way of defining moral relativism defines moral relativism negatively as being *not* moral absolutism. Since there are three distinct forms of moral absolutism, this way of getting into the issue of moral relativism yields three forms of moral relativism: first, there is moral relativism understood as saying there are *no* moral absolutes; second, there is moral relativism understood as saying there is *no* absolute moral standard; and, third, there is moral relativism understood as saying that there are *no* exceptionless moral norms. These three forms of moral relativism are different from one another, and each is different from subjectivism and cultural moral relativism.

And then I introduced an important distinction between the *determining* type of moral relativism and the *varying* type. Subjectivism and cultural moral relativism are determining types of moral relativism, for each says what determines moral rightness—and for whom. The varying type does not in itself say what determines moral rightness; it leaves this open. It says what is right or wrong can, sometimes, vary from person to person or from society to society. So, again using Herodotus' example, while it is right for the Greeks to burn the bodies of their fathers, it would be wrong for the Callatians to burn the bodies of *their* fathers; and similarly while, other things being equal, it is wrong for me not to do a certain thing for someone when I promised I would, it is not wrong for someone else, who made no such promise, not to do that thing. In this precise sense the varying type of moral relativism denies that there is but one true morality. And in this way the varying type of moral relativism accommodates the intuition of many that sometimes what is right for one person is wrong for another, without leading us on to either subjectivism or cultural moral relativism.

Yusuf: Let me add what I see is an important point, although it may be implicit in Vishnu's summary. It's a point we talked about and agreed on, I think. There may be moral universals, there may even be moral absolutes, and yet the proper observance of them is relative. So, to revert to my earlier example, marital fidelity may be a moral universal, and even a moral absolute—so that it is morally binding on all those in a marital relationship to be faithful—but the way marital fidelity is observed may be relative to a culture—so that having more than one wife is forbidden and wrong in one culture while being allowed and right in another.

Jerry: Yes, I think we agreed on this. At least it seems right to me. I would underline another point that Vishnu left implicit in his summary. Say that the varying type of moral relativism is correct. That does not mean that subjectivism or cultural moral relativism is correct. And say that both subjectivism and cultural moral relativism are proved wrong, as I believe they can be. Still, the varying type of moral relativism can be correct.

Maria: And we saw that the varying type of moral relativism does not rule out there being an absolute standard. Specifically it allows that God's law is the absolute standard. It is just that there can be different appropriate ways of observing God's law, so that in some Jewish communities keeping kosher is required, although Christians are not required to keep kosher in order to follow God's law. However, I do not think that we can use Yusuf's example of varying forms of marital fidelity here. Many of those in my church would not agree that polygamy is an acceptable way of following God's law, not for anyone.

Yusuf: I do not doubt what you say about those in your church, Maria. At the same time many Muslims are very clear that having more than one wife is perfectly in accord with God's law. And some enlightened Islamic thinkers, like myself, would allow that the Christian monogamous and Islamic polygamous marital relationships are two acceptable ways of following God's law.

Andrew: So some issues remain. Thank you, Vishnu, for that summary and retrospective look at the ground we have covered. You know, it might be interesting to take all that we have talked about in our discussions over these past weeks back to those examples of strange or upsetting practices in other cultures that each of us presented that first night. I'll start, but let me shift from the example I presented that evening—the American practice of driving two blocks to the store instead of walking—to another example I later presented, that of my friend Paul thinking that the way Americans greeted him on the street was unfriendly. Paul's reaction had two phases. First, he reacted to what is strange in another culture's ways and had the perception of moral difference, and the sense that this strange way of doing something is wrong. Then when he gained some familiarity with American culture and ethnocentrism was overcome, he had a corrected perception of a shared value in a different expression, and so of a basic moral agreement. Since his arrival in America the way Paul greets people has become more subdued. He is still friendly, but in a more American way.

Jerry: So in this case a shared moral value was discovered—being friendly—and Paul identified two different cultural expressions of that value. Moreover, since he was in America, he adopted the American expression of that value as perfectly all right. But in another case there could be a noteworthy difference. Recall Herodotus again. Despite their different ways of honoring their dead fathers, the Greeks and Callatians both shared that moral value, and a Greek who had overcome ethnocentrism could recognize that he shared this value with the Callatians. At the same time the Greeks doubtlessly would still find eating their fathers—the Callatian expression of this value—deeply disgusting and wrong for *them* to do.

Sam: My example was infanticide. When I presented it that first night of our discussion I found the practice cruel and wrong. In the light of what we have seen about Inuit culture, I now see that the Inuit and we—we in American mainstream culture—share the value, the moral value, of maintaining the family; and Inuit parents in their traditional culture did what they had to do to preserve the family and care for as many children as they could. They were, in a relevant moral sense, doing the same thing Americans or Europeans do when they care for their families. I see all of this, although I still feel some internal resistance to saying that the Inuit did what was right. I think that their expression of this shared moral value *may* be wrong.

Yusuf: Yes, one might encounter a practice in another culture, realize it exemplifies a shared moral value, but not be able to judge if it is not only a different but also a morally right expression of a shared moral value *or* something that is simply wrong. This seems to characterize Sam's reaction to Inuit infanticide. It also characterizes my reaction to the way American women dress. There is of course some standard for modesty in dress in America, but it is very different from the standard in Pakistan. It is so different that I think the American standard may not qualify as proper modesty at all. I say "may not qualify as proper modesty," because, like Sam, I cannot judge.

Maria: My example provides another variation. My example was people *not* eating pork and *not* eating beef. In my family we would gather for Saturday morning breakfast and on other occasions and have really good food, like *chorizo* with potatoes and eggs, or *tamales*. It was a time of family intimacy, where feelings and love were communicated. But without pork and beef we wouldn't have those dishes to enjoy or the occasion for our family gathering. I appreciated that within other cultures, and within the American mainstream culture, there are traditional Jews, Muslims, and Hindus who do not eat pork or beef. But I found it hard to imagine anything in those cultural traditions that could approach the happy occasions in my family. Sarah came to my rescue by telling me about Shabbat dinners in her household. From her description of those family dinners I could see that there was the same occasion for family intimacy in the midst of good food. It is just that the food was different. What we saw, I came to appreciate, was that her family and my family valued the same thing—family intimacy—but that its expression was a little different, at least as far as the food was concerned. Here is the variation. I am very clear that Sarah's family and my family follow different expressions of the same value. However, while it is allowable for me and my family to eat the ratzelech that Sarah described, since Sarah and her family keep kosher it would be wrong for her and her family to eat *chorizo con papas y huevos*,

Sarah: There is another kind of moral reaction that is more categorical: a lasting perception that what is done in other cultures really is wrong and should not be practiced even in that society. Jerry's reaction to honor killing is of this kind. Others have had this reaction to slavery, to anti-Semitism, and to the persecution of minorities when they are encountered in cultures other than their own.

Jerry: Yes, that is my reaction to honor killing.

Zainab: And it is my reaction to both honor killing and female genital mutilation. It was examples of this sort that figured in those arguments against cultural moral relativism that Jerry and I presented.

Jerry: So far, in thinking back on the examples each of us presented that first night, we have identified moral reactions. But pretty clearly some of our examples elicit nonmoral reactions. My example of people standing very close in conversation, as is done in Italy, is such an example. This is simply a difference in perceived custom. One might say here, "When in Rome do as the Romans do." However, I think that if I were in Rome in conversation with an Italian I would want to have a little more conversational distance than the Romans like, in order to feel comfortable. By way of contrast I would have no discomfort in calling my Italian hosts "Signor" and "Signora," which I have read is what is expected in Italy, as opposed to American informality. These are matters of good manners and, like Vishnu's using the wrong fork for the fish course, are not in themselves moral matters. Not following or following good manners, of course, can take on moral significance, as we saw. If not following good manners would give offense, then, morally, one should follow what local custom defines as good manners. And if following customary good manners worked some kind of social injustice, then, morally, one should not follow good manners. But the example of standing close in conversation that I presented in itself has no moral dimension that I can see.

Zainab: Another kind of nonmoral reaction arises from what are simple differences in taste. Given the dietary laws of Judaism and Islam, it is wrong for Sarah and me to eat insects, just as it is wrong for us to eat pork, except that grasshoppers are allowed in Islam. Take away the prohibitions of the dietary laws of Judaism and Islam, and she and I, like many others, would still find the eating of insects repellant. It is something that might make those in this country cry out "Ick!" However, while we find eating insects repellant and we may feel queasy or worse—setting aside our religious dietary laws—our reaction is not one of moral disapproval.

Andrew: Another kind of reaction is that what is encountered is weird or disquieting, but only that. Vishnu's reaction to the use of skull cups in Buddhist rituals in Tibet may be of this sort; and what might be a Buddhist's reaction— or a Jewish or Muslim reaction—to the Christian liturgy for Holy Communion may be of this sort. In itself this is not a moral reaction. It is a reaction to what one finds unfamiliar and even upsetting, but not *morally* upsetting.

Vishnu: I would like to supply one other kind of reaction, one that is not represented in our offered examples. It is the perception that what is done in other cultures is right and morally *better* than in our culture. Like several of us around this table I have more than one culture. I am Indian. I am British. And now I am also American. I think that some of the American cultural ways are better—morally better—than the ways of my Indian culture. I have in mind the treatment of women in India, especially widows. At the same time, I think that some of the ways I observe in American culture are morally deficient. I must confess I am surprised and even shocked at the pervasive racial discrimination I find in my American culture. Since I am a person of color I experience it myself, but not as much as black Americans, maybe because I am often perceived as "foreign." By way of contrast I think of French or Parisian culture as it was in the early and mid-twentieth century. It was more welcoming to black Americans than their native America, so much so that a number of black American musicians and writers went to France to live in the twentieth century. James Baldwin was one. Josephine Baker, a dancer in the1920s and 30s and later was another. When she came back to New York in 1936, she was disgusted by the racism, and she returned to France. Of course, this is not to say that France is or was free of racial discrimination, but more than one black American artist found an acceptance in Paris that was lacking in his or her home country.

Sam: Was this difference between French and American culture a difference in moral belief? Was there a belief in American culture that racial discrimination was morally acceptable and a belief in French culture that it was wrong?

Vishnu: There may be more involved than moral belief. In France there may have been a greater appreciation of the esthetic power of black American artists than they enjoyed at home. And I am not saying that there is no racial discrimination in France. Recently there have been bitter complaints about discrimination in hiring in France by those of North African descent. But when we compare the French acceptance of black American artists in the twentieth century with the discrimination they experienced in America, there may have been a difference in moral belief. It would not be a difference in *proclaimed* belief. However, more than one thinker has said that what we truly believe is expressed in our behavior.

Andrew: And we might observe that in more recent years a number of African musicians have found France to be hospitable.

So there is a range of reactions in the examples we have presented. On the one hand some reactions are not moral at all. Some of these nonmoral reactions come from a confrontation with a different culture's manners or customs that make us feel uncomfortable; still we feel that we could observe such customs if we were to visit such a culture. Here there is no moral judgment. Some reactions are matters of taste, probably having a lot to do with what we are used to. Here we may find that what is strange to us is "icky" or repellant, but no moral judgment is invited. And some of these nonmoral reactions are reactions to what seems weird to us, as to the language and symbolism in religious practices in religions other than our own. On the other hand in some of our examples there is a moral reaction. One reaction is that some practice found in another culture is morally wrong regardless of what the culture says. Another reaction is that it *may be* wrong, and we cannot judge. Another reaction that we have seen in our discussion, even if not in reactions to our original examples, is that some practice is all right, or even morally required, in one society, but wrong in another. And also sometimes— at least sometimes—the reaction can be that the way a thing is done in another culture is morally *better* than the way it is done in our own culture.

Vishnu: Thank you, Andrew. But now it is getting late. Perhaps we should end.

Sam: Before we break up, Sarah and I have an announcement.

Sarah: Sam and I would like to announce our engagement.

Jerry and Vishnu: Congratulations!

Zainab, Maria, Yusuf, and Andrew: Congratulations!

Sarah: You are all invited to our announcement party at my parents' house next Saturday.

Jerry, Vishnu, Zainab, Maria, Yusuf, and Andrew: We'll be there!

[There is a loud knock on the door, and Sam goes to the door and opens it.]

Sam: Shawn! Hello, come in.

Shawn: Thanks, man. Hey, I see the party is still going on. Don't let me interrupt.

[There is an even louder knock at the door. Sam goes to the door, but does not open it.]

Sam: Who's there?

A voice from the other side of the door: It's the police!

Notes

CHAPTER 1

The film *The Decision* is fictional.

Jean-Paul Sartre was a French philosopher, playwright, and novelist. He wrote *Existentialism is a Humanism* in 1946 in order to clarify his philosophy of existentialism.

Pope Benedict XVI issued this warning against relativism in a homily, or sermon, that he preached in April 2005 just before he was elected pope by the conclave of cardinals.

Jerry's definition of "objective" captures a primary meaning of this term. Other definitions are possible. David Wong identifies a number of claims that philosophers might have in mind when they call morality objective. David B. Wong, *Moral Relativity* (Berkeley: University of California Press, 1984), p. 1.

The passage in Sartre's *Existentialism is a Humanism* that Jerry and Vishnu have in mind, and from which Vishnu quotes, is this:

> When we say that man chooses himself, we do mean that every one of us must choose himself; but by that we also mean that in choosing for himself he chooses for all men. For in effect, of all the actions a man may take in order to create himself as he wills to be, there is not one which is not creative, at the same time, of an image of man as he

believes he ought to be. To choose between this or that is at the same time to affirm the value of that which is chosen; for we are unable ever to choose the worse. What we choose is always the better, and nothing can be better for us unless it is better for all.

Jean-Paul Sartre, *Existentialism is a Humanism*, trans. Philip Mairet, in *Existentialism from Dostoevsky to Sartre*, ed. Walter Kaufmann (New York: Meridian/The New American Library, 1975), p. 350.

Sartre's argument has been commented on by Mary Warnock in her *Existentialist Ethics* (London: Macmillan/St. Martin's, 1967), pp. 39–40. She judges it to be "rather dubious."

In the art and rituals of Vajrayana Buddhism, skull cups have various symbolic meanings. Among other things they are a reminder of death and the transitory nature of life. The representations of Kali to which Vishnu refers show her in a fierce aspect. The "European religious painting" he mentions is Francisco de Zurburán's *St. Francis Kneeling* in the National Gallery, London.

When Andrew observes that in the New Testament Jesus says that those who eat his flesh and drink his blood will have eternal life, he is referring to the book of John 6:54.

Sarah does not mention a source, but the consumption of blood is forbidden in the Torah in Leviticus 7:26–27 and 17:10–14. The Torah consists of the Five Books of Moses, the first five books of the Jewish Bible, or Tanakh, and of the Christian Bible.

Although Zainab does not name a Qur'anic source, the eating of blood is forbidden in the Qur'an 6:145. The Qur'an (or Koran) is the sacred book or scripture of Islam.

When Zainab says that Islamic scholars have condemned the practice of honor killing she may have in mind the condemnation of honor killing as un-Islamic by Ayatollah Ali Khamenei, the highest Islamic authority in Iran and the Supreme Leader of Iran.

Ruth Benedict and Melville J. Herskovits were leading exponents of cultural relativism in the twentieth century. John Cook in *Morality and Cultural Differences* (Oxford: Oxford University Press, 1999) argues that Benedict and Herskovits did not really follow their teacher Franz Boas in holding cultural relativism.

Melville J. Herskovits formulated and defended cultural relativism in "Cultural Relativism and Cultural Values," chap. 19 of *Cultural Anthropology* (New York: Knopf, 1955), pp. 348–66. *Cultural Anthropology* was first published in 1947.

The concerns that Jerry raises about the "chaos" of subjectivism are related to some of Bernard Williams' reflections in "Subjectivism: First Thoughts" and "Subjectivism: Further Thoughts" in *Morality: An Introduction to Ethics* (New York: Harper & Row, 1972).

The argument in favor of cultural moral relativism that Vishnu draws to the attention of the group is considered and criticized by Walter T. Stace in "Ethical Relativity (I)," in *The Concept of Morals* (New York: Macmillan, 1962), pp. 13–16, and by James Rachels in "The Challenge of Cultural Relativism," chap. 2 of *The Elements of Moral Philosophy*, 4th edition (Boston: McGraw-Hill, 2003), pp. 19–21. Rachels calls it "The Cultural Differences Argument."

Herodotus' account of the funeral practices of the Greeks and the Callatians is in *Ethical Relativism*, ed. John Ladd (Belmont, CA: Wadsworth Publishing Company, 1973), p. 12.

CHAPTER 2

Maria's concern about which society or culture determines moral rightness for her is related to Walter Stace's comments about the lack of a definition of "social group" and the problem this causes for ethical relativity or cultural moral relativism. Walter T. Stace, "Ethical Relativity (II)," in *The Concept of Morals*, p. 52.

Terence Turner recounts how Herskovits wrote the statement on behalf of the American Anthropological Association Executive Board objecting to the United Nations Universal Declaration of Human Rights in "Human Rights, Human Difference: Anthropology's Contribution to an Emancipatory Cultural Politics," *Journal of Anthropological Research*, 53, no. 3 (Fall 1997): 277–78.

Elizabeth M. Zechenter argues for "human rights universalism" in her "In the Name of Culture: Cultural Relativism and the Abuse of the Individual," *Journal of Anthropological Research*, 53, no. 3 (Fall 1997): 319–47.

Carole Nagengast, discusses the right to bodily integrity in "Women, Minorities, and Indigenous Peoples: Universalism and Cultural Relativity," *Journal of Anthropological Research*, 53, no. 3 (Fall 1997): 360. While she does not straightforwardly advocate such a right, she mentions several other authors who do, such as, B. Allen in *Rape Warfare: The Hidden Genocide in Bosnia-Herzegovina and Croatia* (Minneapolis: University of Minnesota Press, 1996).

James Rachels discusses the issue of judging the practices of other cultures to be wrong or "undesirable" in "The Challenge of Cultural Relativism" in *The Elements of Moral Philosophy*, pp. 26–27. His example is what Zainab refers to as "female genital mutilation," and Rachels on p. 28 goes on to suggest as a standard for evaluating a cultural practice, not the violation of human rights, but the promotion or hindrance of the welfare of the people affected. The standard to which Rachels appeals is one of the "higher standards" named by Vishnu at the beginning of chapter 3.

The arguments offered by Jerry and Zainab are variants of arguments to be found in Walter T. Stace, "Ethical Relativity (II)," in *The Concept of Morals*, pp. 45–48 and in James Rachels, "The Challenge of Cultural Relativism," in *The Elements of Moral Philosophy*, pp. 21–23.

Riffat Hasan is among those Muslim thinkers who maintain that the Qur'an affirms the rights of women. She is the founder of The International Network for the Rights of Female Victims of Violence in Pakistan.

Sati (or suttee) was accepted in India for centuries. It was made illegal by the British in 1829, but the custom did not die out immediately. Today the practice of sati in India is rare. However there remains a weakening but general negative attitude toward widows, who in the historical Hindu tradition were considered a bad omen. Vasudha Narayanan, "The Hindu Tradition," chap. 1 of *World Religions: Eastern Traditions*, 2nd edition, ed. Willard G. Oxtoby (Oxford and New York: Oxford University Press, 2002), pp. 100–102.

CHAPTER 3

Before giving her description of the different forms that wearing hijab can take for women in the Muslim world, Zainab says that in Islam modesty in dress is required of both men and women. She is referring to the Qur'an 24:30–31.

Jerry's made-up example is indeed realistic, as he says. In some West African countries, even in the twenty-first century, parents in desperate poverty sell their children to traffickers in the hope that they will find a paying job. Often they end up as virtual slaves.

Walter Stace allows that the principle "When in Rome do as the Romans do" is a good rule in etiquette, as opposed to morality. Walter T. Stace, "Ethical Relativity (II)," in *The Concept of Morals*, pp. 52–53. Bernard Williams observes that this principle "is at best a principle of etiquette." Bernard Williams, "Interlude: Relativism," in *Morality: An Introduction to Ethics*, p. 24.

CHAPTER 4

James Rachels in "The Challenge of Cultural Relativism," in *The Elements of Moral Philosophy*, p. 19, and Bernard Williams in "Interlude: Relativism," in *Morality: An Introduction to Ethics*, pp. 20–21, see cultural moral relativism as urging tolerance toward other societies as an attitude that all should adopt. Williams on p. 21 of "Interlude: Relativism" speaks of a "logically unhappy attachment of a nonrelative morality of toleration" to "a view of morality as relative," that is, to cultural moral relativism.

The Hitler Youth was a Nazi youth organization for boys and girls from the ages of six to eighteen. It came to have more than seven million members. William L. Shirer describes the Hitler Youth in *The Rise and Fall of the Third Reich* (New York: Simon and Schuster, 1960), pp. 252–56.

Herskovits comments on functionality as a test for evaluating family arrangements and the functional value of the Dahomean family unit in "Cultural Relativism and Cultural Values," in *Cultural Anthropology*, pp. 348–49. Bernard Williams sees functionality as one of the "three propositions" of cultural moral relativism in "Interlude: Relativism," in *Morality: An Introduction to Ethics*, p. 20.

Vishnu's two characterizations of ethnocentrism are adapted from William Graham Sumner's definition in "Folkways," in *Ethical Relativism*, ed. John Ladd, p. 28 and from Herskovits' definition in Melville J. Herskovits, "Cultural Relativism and Cultural Values," *Cultural Anthropology*, p. 356.

Vilhjálmur Stefánsson comments that Inuits lightly make and easily break promises in *My Life with the Eskimo* (New York: Collier Books, 1913), pp. 270–71. Cf. Peter Freuchen, *Book of the Eskimos* (Cleveland and New York: The World Publishing Company, 1961), p. 189.

Peter Freuchen describes examples of "wife sharing" in Inuit culture and the circumstances that surround them in Peter Freuchen, *Book of the Eskimos*, pp. 79–84.

Freuchen describes the Inuit custom of family members assisting the aged to commit suicide by hanging in Peter Freuchen, *Book of the Eskimos*, pp. 194–95; Freuchen recounts that in other instances an aged Inuit might ask a family member to stab him or her and bring on death that way. Also the death of the aged was brought about by exposure to the cold, as by leaving an old person in a snow house, or in an open snow field, which was done if the group was traveling. E. Adamson Hoebel, *The Law of Primitive Man* (Cambridge, MA: Harvard University Press, 1964), p. 77.

When Jerry points out that some argue that assisted suicide is humane in cases where the alternative is untreatable pain he may have in mind the position held by Dr. Jack Kevorkian, which Kevorkian argues for in his *Prescription: Medicide* (Buffalo, NY: Prometheus Books, 1991).

Vishnu's example of the Dinka people's ceremonial burial of the spear-master is discussed by John Kekes in *The Morality of Pluralism* (Princeton: Princeton University Press, 1993), pp. 125ff. Kekes's source is Godfrey Lienhardt, *Divinity and Experience: The Religion of the Dinka* (Oxford: Clarendon Press, 1961), pp. 206–211, 299–319.

Vishnu's point citing the distinction between beliefs and values, and Jerry's point about the importance of circumstances, are derived from James Rachels' discussion in "The Challenge of Cultural Relativism" in *The Elements of Moral Philosophy*, as is the example of Inuit infanticide. Rachels argues that differences in behavior between cultures or societies may stem from differences in"religious and factual beliefs" and "differences in the physical circumstances in which they must live" and not from differences in values on pp. 23–24; he considers Inuit infanticide on pp. 24–25. Rachels also comments that female Inuit infants are more often killed than male infants. He cites two reasons: males, as hunters, are the primary food providers, and, second, since there is a higher mortality rate among younger males (because hunting is so dangerous), killing female babies helps to keep the number of young men comparable to the number of young women. Rachels is drawing upon anthropological findings discussed by E. Adamson Hoebel, *The Law of Primitive Man*, pp. 74–76.

Clyde Kluckhorn is among those anthropologists who recognize moral universals. The examples of moral universals cited by Jerry are taken from Clyde Kluckhorn, "Ethical Relativity: *Sic et Non*," in *Ethical Relativism*, ed. John Ladd, p. 89.

Herskovits acknowledges that morality is universal in the sense that it is found in some form in all cultures in Melville J. Herskovits, "Cultural Relativism and Cultural Values," in *Cultural Anthropology*, p. 364.

The distinction between moral universals and moral absolutes that Vishnu introduces owes something to Paul Taylor's distinction between "factual universals" and "moral absolutes." Paul Taylor, "Social Science and Ethical Relativism" in *Ethical Relativism*, ed. John Ladd, pp. 103, 104. Walter Stace too recognizes a distinction between universals and absolutes. Walter T. Stace, "Ethical Relativity (II)," in *The Concept of Morals*, p. 67. And Herskovits distinguishes between moral absolutes and universals in his sense of "universals." Melville J. Herskovits, "Cultural Relativism and Cultural Values," in *Cultural Anthropology*, p. 364. Clyde Kluckhorn said that "we must not glibly equate universals with absolutes." Clyde Kluckhorn, "Ethical Relativity: *Sic et Non*," in *Ethical Relativism*, ed. John Ladd, p. 90.

Herskovits comments on how wives in the Dahomean family arrangement urged their husbands to take a second wife in Melville J. Herskovits, "Cultural Relativism and Cultural Values," in *Cultural Anthropology*, p. 349. Mary H. Kingsley observes that African women say, "The more wives the less work," in *Travels in West Africa* (New York: Dover, 2003), p. 212. Originally published in 1897.

Freuchen observes that married Inuits "are generally very devoted to each other and remain faithful to each other throughout life." Peter Freuchen, *Book of the Eskimos*, p. 81.

CHAPTER 5

Robert Redfield recounts the episode that Vishnu describes and observes that "morality is both relative and universal" in "The Universally Human and the Culturally Variable," in *Ethical Relativism*, ed. John Ladd, p. 142.

The case that Maria presents of the difficult moral situation that the Mendozas faced and the moral decision that they made is a fictional case.

Vishnu's point about the presence of moral regret in the cases of the fire captain's and the Mendozas' moral decisions is related to Bernard Williams' observation that there is a place for understandable and proper regret in "the most extreme cases of moral conflict." Bernard Williams, "Ethical Consistency," in *Problems of the Self* (London: Cambridge University Press, 1973), pp. 173–74.

Vishnu's comments on "good lives" owe much to John Kekes's argument that there are various possible good lives. John Kekes, *The Morality of Pluralism*.

CHAPTER 6

John Stuart Mill's absolute moral standard, which Sam mentions and Sarah describes, is Mill's "greatest happiness principle." It is defended by Mill in his *Utilitarianism*. Originally published in 1861.

Jerry's formulation of Immanuel Kant's absolute standard is based on Kant's "categorical imperative," which Kant promulgated in his *Groundwork of the Metaphysic of Morals*. Originally published in 1785.

Kant's understanding of moral duty, such as the duty not to lie, made moral norms exceptionless. Pope John Paul II in his 1993 encyclical *Veritatis Splendor* (The Splendor of Truth) affirmed "universal and unchanging moral norms." By "universal" norms he apparently meant *universally binding* norms, or "moral absolutes" in the sense Vishnu introduced; and by "unchanging" norms he apparently meant that they admitted of no exceptions or are exceptionless. Although it is possible, as Vishnu points out, to affirm moral absolutism by affirming (1) moral absolutes, while rejecting (2) an absolute standard and (3) exceptionless moral norms, it is also possible to accept (1) and (3) together, as Pope John Paul II does in what is quoted, or to accept (1) and (2) together or (1), (2), and (3) together, as Kant did and as Pope John Paul II almost certainly did. John Stuart Mill held (2) the existence of an absolute standard while rejecting (3) exceptionless moral norms. For Mill, moral norms, like "It is wrong to lie," are secondary principles and are overruled whenever the act in question produces the most happiness.

Walter Stace, who thought of religion, or at least Christianity, as providing an absolute standard in the form of the will of God expressed in God's commands, thought it no longer viable to appeal to God as the source of an absolute standard "in an age of widespread religious skepticism." Walter T. Stace, "Ethical Relativity (I)" in *The Concept of Morals*, pp. 6, 8. Although Vishnu does not mention it, in a strong strain of Christian thought going back at least to St. Thomas Aquinas the idea that God's commands constituted; the absolute standard for moral rightness and wrongness, in the sense that right actions are right *because* God commands them and wrong actions are wrong *because* they are counter to God's commands or God commands that they not be done, was rejected. Moral absolutism was not denied by these Christian thinkers, nor did they deny that God's law or moral order was the absolute moral standard. But they did not see God's commands per se as being what *makes* right actions right or wrong actions wrong.

The "agreement" form of moral relativism to which Vishnu refers is defended by Gilbert Harman in "Moral Relativism Defended" in *Relativism: Cognitive and Moral*, eds. Jack W. Meiland and Michael Krausz (Notre Dame, IN: University of Notre Dame Press, 1982). Harman returns to this form of relativism in his "Moral Relativism" in Gilbert Harman and Judith Jarvis Thomson, *Moral Relativism and Moral Objectivity* (Cambridge, MA and Oxford: Blackwell, 1996).

Vishnu in presenting the "varying type" of moral relativism, and in characterizing it as holding that there is no single true morality, is drawing upon the thinking of David Wong. David Wong calls "relativists" those who deny "there is a single true morality" and "usually," he says, one or more of the claims made by those who claim that morality is "objective" (in the sense of "objective" that he identifies, as opposed to Jerry's sense). For Wong, then, the essential claim made by moral relativists is that there is no single true morality. David B. Wong, *Moral Relativism* (Berkeley and Los Angeles: University of California Press, 1984), pp. 1, 4.

When Vishnu mentions Socrates' view about what we owe the state we live in, he has in mind the view that Socrates argues for in the *Crito*, one of the Socratic dialogues written by Plato. Socrates argues that all those who live in Athens, and by extension in any state, enjoying the protection of the laws owe it to the state to obey its laws.

The point that Zainab makes about reacting to something by saying "Ick!" is related to the point that Michael Nava and Robert Dawidoff make about the "Ick Factor." However what Nava and Dawidoff mean by the "Ick Factor" is a "revulsion [that] equates distaste with immorality," while Zainab is making the point that a reaction of distaste is not in itself a reaction of moral disapproval. Michael Nava and Robert Dawidoff, *Created Equal: Why Gay Rights Matter to America* (New York: St. Martin's Press, 1994), p. 5.

When Vishnu refers to thinkers who have held that what we truly believe is expressed in our behavior, he may have in mind William James. William James in "The Will to Believe," says in an important footnote that "belief is measured by action." William James, "The Will to Believe," in *Essays in Pragmatism*, ed. Albury Castell (New York: Hafner Press, 1948), p. 108n4.

Bibliography

Castell, Albury, ed. *Essays in Pragmatism*. New York: Hafner Press, 1948.

Cook, John. *Morality and Cultural Differences*. Oxford: Oxford University Press, 1999.

Freuchen, Peter. *Book of the Eskimos*. Cleveland and New York: The World Publishing Company, 1961.

Harman, Gilbert. "Moral Relativism Defended." In *Relativism: Cognitive and Moral*, eds. Jack W. Meiland and Michael Krausz. Notre Dame, IN: University of Notre Dame Press, 1982.

Harman, Gilbert, and Judith Jarvis Thomson. *Moral Relativism and Moral Objectivity*. Cambridge, MA and Oxford: Blackwell, 1996.

Herskovits, Melville J., "Cultural Relativism and Cultural Values." In *Cultural Anthropology*. New York: Knopf, 1955, pp. 348–66.

Hoebel, E. Adamson. *The Law of Primitive Man*. Cambridge, MA: Harvard University Press, 1964.

James, William. "The Will to Believe." In *Essays in Pragmatism*, ed. Albury Castell. New York: Hafner Press, 1948.

Kant, Immanuel. *Groundwork of the Metaphysic of Morals*. 1785.

Kekes, John. *The Morality of Pluralism*. Princeton, NJ: Princeton University Press, 1993, pp. 125ff.

Kevorkian, Jack. *Prescription: Medicide*. Buffalo, NY: Prometheus Books, 1991.

Kingsley, Mary H. *Travels in West Africa*. New York: Dover, 2003.

Kluckhorn, Clyde. "Ethical Relativity: *Sic et Non*." In *Ethical Relativism*, ed. John Ladd. Belmont, CA: Wadsworth Publishing Company, 1973.

Ladd, John, ed. *Ethical Relativism*. Belmont, CA: Wadsworth Publishing Company, 1973.

Lienhardt, Godfrey. *Divinity and Experience: The Religion of the Dinka*. Oxford: Clarendon Press, 1961.

Mill, John Stuart. *Utilitarianism*. 1861.

Nagengast, Carole. "Women, Minorities, and Indigenous Peoples: Universalism and Cultural Relativity." *Journal of Anthropological Research* 53, no. 3 (Fall 1997): 360.

Narayanan, Vasudha. "The Hindu Tradition." *World Religions: Eastern Traditions*, 2nd edition, ed, Willard G. Oxtoby. New York: Oxford University Press, 2002.

Nava, Michael, and Robert Dawidoff. *Created Equal: Why Gay Rights Matter to America*. New York: St. Martin's Press, 1994.

Pope John Paul II. *Veritatis Splendor* (The Splendor of Truth). 1993.

Rachels, James. "The Challenge of Cultural Relativism." In *The Elements of Moral Philosophy*, 4th edition. Boston: McGraw-Hill, 2003.

Redfield, Robert. "The Universally Human and the Culturally Variable." In *Ethical Relativism*, ed. John Ladd. Belmont, CA: Wadsworth Publishing Company, 1973, p.142.

Sartre, Jean-Paul. *Existentialism is a Humanism*. Trans. Philip Mairet. In *Existentialism from Dostoevsky to Sartre*, ed. Walter Kaufmann. New York: Meridian/The New American Library, 1975, p. 350.

Shirer, William L. *The Rise and Fall of the Third Reich*. New York: Simon and Schuster, 1960, pp. 252–56.

Socrates. *Crito*.

Stace, Walter T. "Ethical Relativity (I)." In *The Concept of Morals*. New York: Macmillan, 1962.

Stace, Walter T. "Ethical Relativity (II)." In *The Concept of Morals*. New York: Macmillan, 1962.

Stefánsson, Vilhjálmur. *My Life with the Eskimo*. New York: Collier Books, 1913.

Sumner, William Graham. "Folkways." In *Ethical Relativism*, ed. John Ladd. Belmont, CA: Wadsworth Publishing Company, 1973, p. 28.

Taylor, Paul. "Social Science and Ethical Relativism." In *Ethical Relativism*, ed. John Ladd. Belmont, CA: Wadsworth Publishing Company, 1973.

Turner, Terence. "Human Rights, Human Difference: Anthropology's Contribution to an Emancipatory Cultural Politics." *Journal of Anthropological Research* 53, no. 3 (Fall 1997): 277–78.

Warnock, Mary. *Existentialist Ethics*. London: Macmillan/St. Martin's, 1967, pp. 39–40.

Williams, Bernard. "Ethical Consistency." In *Problems of the Self*. London: Cambridge University Press, 1973.

Williams, Bernard. "Interlude: Relativism." In *Morality: An Introduction to Ethics*. New York: Harper & Row, 1972.

Williams, Bernard. "Subjectivism: First Thoughts." In *Morality: An Introduction to Ethics*. New York: Harper & Row, 1972.

Williams, Bernard. "Subjectivism: Further Thoughts." In *Morality: An Introduction to Ethics*. New York: Harper & Row, 1972.

Wong, David B. *Moral Relativism*. Berkeley: University of California Press, 1984.

Zechenter, Elizabeth M. "In the Name of Culture: Cultural Relativism and the Abuse of the Individual." *Journal of Anthropological Research* 53, no. 3 (Fall 1997): 319–47.

Index

About the Author

J. Kellenberger has taught philosophy for many years at California State University, Northridge, and is the author of articles and books in philosophy of religion and philosophical ethics. Among his previous books is *Moral Relativism, Moral Diversity, and Human Relationships*.